Cambridge Elements ≡

Elements in Ethics
edited by
Ben Eggleston
University of Kansas
Dale E. Miller
Old Dominion University, Virginia

ARISTOTLE'S ETHICS

Nicomachean and *Eudemian* Themes

Paula Gottlieb
University of Wisconsin, Madison

CAMBRIDGE
UNIVERSITY PRESS

CAMBRIDGE
UNIVERSITY PRESS

University Printing House, Cambridge CB2 8BS, United Kingdom

One Liberty Plaza, 20th Floor, New York, NY 10006, USA

477 Williamstown Road, Port Melbourne, VIC 3207, Australia

314–321, 3rd Floor, Plot 3, Splendor Forum, Jasola District Centre,
New Delhi – 110025, India

103 Penang Road, #05–06/07, Visioncrest Commercial, Singapore 238467

Cambridge University Press is part of the University of Cambridge.

It furthers the University's mission by disseminating knowledge in the pursuit of
education, learning, and research at the highest international levels of excellence.

www.cambridge.org
Information on this title: www.cambridge.org/9781108706575
DOI: 10.1017/9781108588034

First published 2022

A catalogue record for this publication is available from the British Library.

ISBN 978-1-108-70657-5 Paperback
ISSN 2516-4031 (online)
ISSN 2516-4023 (print)

Aristotle's Ethics

Nicomachean and *Eudemian* Themes

Elements in Ethics

DOI: 10.1017/9781108588034
First published online: May 2022

Paula Gottlieb
University of Wisconsin, Madison

Author for correspondence: Paula Gottlieb, plgottli@wisc.edu

Abstract: This Element is an examination of the philosophical themes presented in Aristotle's *Nicomachean* and *Eudemian Ethics*. Topics include happiness, the voluntary and choice, the doctrine of the mean, particular virtues of character and temperamental means, virtues of thought, *akrasia*, pleasure, friendship, and luck. Special attention has been paid to Aristotle's treatment of virtues of character and thought and their relation to happiness, the reason why Aristotle is the quintessential virtue ethicist. The virtues of character have not received the attention they deserve in most discussions of the relationship between the two treatises.

Keywords: Aristotle, *Nicomachean Ethics*, *Eudemian Ethics*, virtue, happiness

ISBNs: 9781108706575 (PB), 9781108588034 (OC)
ISSNs: 2516-4031 (online), 2516-4023 (print)

Contents

Introduction

Aristotle (384–322 BCE) was born in the small city of Stagira in northern Greece, studied with Plato in Athens, did pioneering work in biology on Lesbos and elsewhere, and founded his own school, the Lyceum, again in Athens.[1] Despite the fact that he wrote for upper-class men, and denigrated women, slaves, and artisans, his general theory about the happy life for human beings is applicable to all.[2] Reading Aristotle in this more inclusive way is conducive to "fair-mindedness" (*epieikeia*), a trait praised by Aristotle himself as justice, but superior.

Aristotle was a prolific writer, composing works on logic, metaphysics, psychology, biology, aesthetics, rhetoric, ethics, and politics. There are three Aristotelian texts about ethics: the *Nicomachean Ethics* (*EN*), the *Eudemian Ethics* (*EE*), and a work of controversial authorship, the *Magna Moralia* (*MM*).[3] There is also the *Protrepticus*, a work that Aristotle probably wrote early on when he attended Plato's Academy.[4] In addition, Aristotle's *Politics* contains material on the happy life that overlaps with Aristotle's ethical works.

I focus on the *Nicomachean* and *Eudemian Ethics*. The *Nicomachean Ethics* is the most famous of Aristotle's ethical works, and has received the lion's share of attention, having clearer manuscripts, and generally being considered the superior and therefore more mature work.[5] In 1978, Anthony Kenny sparked controversy by arguing on stylometric and philosophical grounds that the *Eudemian Ethics* is in fact the superior and later work.[6] Since then there has been the publication of an Oxford Classical Text by Walzer and Mingay (1991) as well as a spate of new translations and commentaries,[7] but there has also been dissatisfaction with the Oxford Classical text. In an unprecedented move,

---

[1] For a fuller account of his life and school, see Natali (2013). Visit youtube for "Aristotle's lagoon," a series on his studies on Lesbos.

[2] See too Ober (2013) and Keyt (2017).

[3] Dirlmeier (1958) argues that the *Magna Moralia* is an authentic work by Aristotle, preceding the *Eudemian* and *Nicomachean Ethics*. Irwin (2019, xv) agrees. Cooper (1999, 195–211 [1973]) disagrees, arguing that the *Magna Moralia* was written by a student of Aristotle who attended a course of lectures before the *Eudemian* and *Nicomachean Ethics*. Rowe (1975) argues that it is a work by a later writer. (Pace Simpson [2013], a further work, *Virtues and Vices*, is considered to be inauthentic.) For more on Aristotle's ethical treatises, see Bobonich (2006).

[4] See Hutchinson and Johnson (2017).

[5] For earlier history and reception of the *Eudemian Ethics*, see Jost (2014) and Rowe (forthcoming). Commentaries and translations of the *Nicomachean Ethics* include, most recently, Natali (1999), Crisp (2000), Sachs (2001), Broadie and Rowe (2002), Taylor (2006), Ross edited by Brown (2009), Reeve (2014), Irwin's third edition (2019), Beresford (2020), and Meyer (forthcoming). Ross (1923) can be found free on the web.

[6] Stylometry is a method of statistical analysis of the Greek terms in each work.

[7] For example, Woods (1992), Kenny (2011), Inwood and Woolf (2013), and Simpson (2013), translating Bekker's (1831) text, and Dalimier (2013) with her own text. The Oxford translation of the *Eudemian Ethics* has been revised to include the common books (Barnes and Kenny 2014).

Oxford University Press is publishing a new Oxford Classical Text, edited by Christopher Rowe.[8]

The chronology of the two works is disputed. Where the author of the *Nicomachean Ethics* seems to be correcting problems in the *Eudemian Ethics*, it may be reasonable to suppose that the *Nicomachean Ethics* is the later work, although further examination may show that the two works are quite consistent after all. Sometimes one work is more expansive on a given topic than the other. Here it is hard to tell whether the shorter treatment was written later, summarizing the longer one, or whether it was written earlier, before a longer treatment was provided. One work may have arguments that the other lacks. This could be for opposing reasons, for example, that they were later found deficient, or because they were added later.

Compounding these difficulties, the *Nicomachean* and *Eudemian Ethics* have three books in common, a surprising fact that I explain further at the beginning of my section on justice, the topic of the first of the common books. (After this introduction I use the terms "*Nicomachean*" and "*Eudemian*" to refer only to the books outside these "common" books.)

It is usual to assume that whichever work has the superior treatment must have been written later. However, while it is heartening to think that authors improve with age, there is no a priori or empirical reason to accept this view. Indeed, in his latest reconsideration of his seminal work on the two treatises, Kenny argues that the similarities and differences between the *Eudemian* and *Nicomachean Ethics* may not be chronological after all, although he rejects the idea that they were written for different audiences (Kenny 2016, 294).[9]

The aim of this Element is not to solve these historical problems, but to highlight important philosophical similarities and differences between the two works, including the common books that may give us greater insight into Aristotle's thinking and serve to provoke further thought.[10] Given the length of this Element, I have not attempted to give a comprehensive account, but I have paid special attention to Aristotle's treatment of virtues of character and thought and their relation to happiness, the reason why Aristotle is considered to be the forefather of modern virtue ethics. The virtues of character have not received the attention they deserve in most discussions of the relationship between the two treatises.

---

[8] For a full explanation of the need for a new Oxford Classical Text, listen to Rowe (2020).

[9] On the issue of different audiences, see the first footnote to the conclusion to this Element.

[10] For an edition of the *Nicomachean Ethics* with parallel passages from the *Eudemian Ethics* (which the editor considered a commentary by a student of Aristotle, Eudemus), see Burnet (1900).

A comment on the texts and translations: I use the Oxford Classical text of the *Nicomachean Ethics* edited by Bywater (1894) and the Oxford Classical Text of the *Eudemian Ethics* edited by Rowe (forthcoming a) (supplemented by Bywater's texts of the "common" books). According to convention, I refer to passages in Aristotle by book, chapter (Roman numerals in the *Nicomachean Ethics*), and Bekker numbers (page, column, and line numbers from Bekker's edition [1831]), with the caveat that the chapter numbers are much later than Aristotle. Translations are my own, although influenced by the translations of others.[11] There is a glossary of key terms following the conclusion.

1 Happiness

Aristotle is often called a eudaemonist because of the importance of *eudaimonia*, or happiness, in his ethics. The term "*eudaimonia*" in Greek suggests that one has a good guardian angel, a *daimōn*, looking after one, and so is simply a matter of luck. In English the term "happiness" usually means "feeling good." Aristotle, by contrast, argues that happiness is not simply a matter of luck, nor is it merely subjective. In Aristotle's view, happiness is up to us to a considerable extent, and people can think that they are happy when they are not. This is important. If the point of studying the *Eudemian* or *Nicomachean Ethics* is to lead a happy life and learn how to bring up others so that they have a happy life too, then happiness must be something that is up to us to a considerable extent, and it cannot be purely subjective.

It has been objected that "*eudaimonia*" should be translated as "flourishing" or "well-being" rather than "happiness" to point out the difference between Aristotle's conception and our own. However, if moderns have merely changed the subject, there would be no disagreement with Aristotle's view, and there is. Aristotle would think it wrong to consider happiness as merely a subjective feeling, although he does not deny that happiness is pleasant.

According to Aristotle, happiness is not just a private matter, but it is also the purview of the art of politics (*politikē*). An individual can achieve happiness only in the context of a society or polis, and an individual cannot achieve happiness by being selfish and aiming to take more of his or her own fair share. According to Aristotle, only virtuous people can be happy, and greed (*pleonexia*) is the motive for the vice of injustice.

I shall first discuss Aristotle's introduction to happiness found in *Nicomachean Ethics* I, and then highlight some similarities and differences to be found in *Eudemian Ethics* I and II. I shall argue that in the bulk of *Nicomachean Ethics* I Aristotle presents three converging approaches to happiness. The

---

[11] On the difficulty of translating Aristotle's ethics, see Gottlieb (2001b).

first approach is a teleological approach, showing that happiness is the highest good or goal (*telos*) of life. The second approach is to examine current views about happiness and those that have something to be said for them (*EN* I 4), known as the method of *endoxa*. The third approach is that of the biologist, examining how happiness is related to the human psyche, the topic of Aristotle's famous function argument (*EN* I 7).

1.1 The Method of *Endoxa*

I shall begin with the second approach, since, as Aristotle says, we should start with what is familiar to us. According to Aristotle, people get their view of happiness from their own way of life. Thus, the hoi polloi think that it is a life of gratification (like the stereotypical life of a tyrant such as Sardanapallus), while others think it is a political life aiming at honor.[12] Yet others think it is a life of contemplation, and still others think that it is the life of money-making aiming at wealth (*EN* I 4).

Aristotle criticizes all the lives except the life of contemplation. He complains that the hoi polloi's life would be a slavish one, only suitable for nonhuman animals. He argues that politicians aim to be honored for their virtue, and so honor is not the ultimate aim. (In the *Eudemian Ethics*, he is more cynical, claiming that most politicians do just aim at honor, and only true statespeople would aim at virtue.) Nevertheless, virtue alone cannot be the whole story, since being virtuous and asleep would not count as a happy life. Nor would being virtuous but suffering the worst misfortunes. Finally, Aristotle argues that the goal of the money-maker's life, wealth, is not choiceworthy for its own sake, but only for the sake of other things.[13]

Aristotle's criticisms of the different ways of life are instructive, presupposing ideas to be found in his two other approaches to happiness, as well as ideas discussed elsewhere in *Nicomachean Ethics* I. Aristotle's criticisms of the life of pure gratification presuppose that autonomous thought is important for the happy life, and that there is something special about a human life that nonhumans lack, assumptions of Aristotle's function argument. The criticisms of the political life presuppose the importance of activity, a crucial aspect of the function argument. They also point to the importance of external goods in

---

[12] "Sardanapallus" is a garbled name for Ashurbanipal, who ruled over the Assyrian empire with ruthless efficiency in the seventh century BCE. He thought of himself as a scholar king, amassing a library of cuneiform tablets which included the epic of Gilgamesh. However, to the Greeks and to the authors of the biblical story of Jonah, his home, Nineveh, was a city of unrivalled debauchery.

[13] In his *Politics*, Aristotle argues that wealth is necessary up to a point, but not beyond (*Pol.* I 9, 10).

addition to virtue, an idea central to the discussion of Solon at the end of the book. Finally, Aristotle's criticisms of wealth as a final goal presupposes a hierarchy of goals, an assumption of Aristotle's teleological approach to happiness.

It is unclear whether these ways of life are supposed to be mutually exclusive or exhaustive. On the face of it, nothing Aristotle says here rules out the view that the different ways of life might be combined, so that a person could enjoy physical pleasure, contemplation, virtuous activity, honor, and money-making, all to a certain degree. We might think that the way of life of the military, artists, musicians, physicians, sportspeople, those who care for others, and the like should be included. In the *Eudemian Ethics*, Aristotle puts artisans with the money-makers. In Aristotle's time, some of these would have been slaves. We shall see that while Aristotle treats the professions of music, medicine, and sport as analogous to being virtuous, in a common book he draws a sharp distinction between these skills (*technai*) and thoughtfulness, the virtue of thought that is required for virtue of character. As for a life of caring for others, Aristotle devotes two books of the *Nicomachean Ethics* and a separate book in the *Eudemian Ethics* to friendship, including family relationships. Again, it is unclear why some combined ways of life would not be possible. Modern scholars debate whether happiness includes a variety of goods and activities and if so, which ones, and whether happiness and the happy life are the same thing.

1.1.1 Aristotle on Plato's Views

Aristotle now turns abruptly to the views of Plato, specifically Plato's discussion of his form of the good and the view that everything that is good is so because of its relationship to just one thing, the form of the good. (Perhaps a student of Plato in the class has had his hand up for all of the preceding lectures.) Even though the Platonic form of the good was introduced by his friends, Aristotle devotes several pages to criticizing it out of reverence for the truth (*EN* I 6). Aristotle's discussion of Plato makes best sense if treated as a dialogue with the master, with Plato's responses understood. Aristotle's first objections to the form of the good rely on his categories, a division of things in the world into ten categories (substances, quantities, qualities, relatives, places, times and more, as explained in an early work, the *Categories*).[14]

---

[14] I follow Ackrill (1972, 17–24) and Irwin (1988, 53), for example, in thinking that Aristotle intends to classify different types of things, not merely different linguistic predicates. The medieval nominalists interpreted the *Categories* differently. See too Frede (1987) and Menn (1995). The Boethian interpretation best fits the present passage. Otherwise, Aristotle's argument against Plato here would be beside the point.

The first argument is rather obscure but is based on the view that the Platonists treat the form of the good as the number one. Since they do not think that there can be forms of members of a series, they should not think that there can be a form for all the numbers either, presumably because each number has essentially the place that it has and this would not be captured by a general form of, say, the number one. Now it follows that there cannot be a form of the good either, according to Aristotle's categories, because good comes in each category, and relatives relate to substances as if in a series.

Aristotle's next argument is easier to follow. According to his account of the categories, what it is to be a substance differs from what it is to be a quality, which differs from what it is to be a quantity, and so on. According to Aristotle, since what makes something good depends on what type of thing it is and so will differ from category to category, there cannot be one thing, "the form of the good," which makes all types of things – a good substance, an opportune moment, the right quantity, and so forth – good. Yet this is precisely what the form of the good is supposed to be.[15]

We must now assume that the Platonist replies that Aristotle's previous arguments are inapplicable because the form of the good refers to something different from a common or garden universal, and this difference is signified by the term "itself" in "the good itself." Aristotle retorts that the term "itself" adds nothing to "good," because (a) the definition of F and the F itself is the same and (b) "eternal" does not add anything to good. For example, a longer-lasting white is no more white than an ephemeral one.

Next Aristotle suggests that a Platonist might reply to his previous criticisms by distinguishing two sorts of goods: those that are good in themselves and those that are (merely) useful. The Platonist is imagined saying that the form of the good only applies to goods in themselves. Aristotle therefore poses the following dilemma: If pleasures, practical wisdom, and so on are goods in themselves, these have different accounts and so cannot partake in one form of the good, but if only the form of the good is a good in itself, it will be useless, presumably because it will not help us understand anything else.

Aristotle now concedes that different goods are not called "good" merely by chance but may derive from one good or be good by analogy. Here the Platonist might respond that if they derive from one good, that must be the form of the good, or if things are analogously good, there must be some aspect according to which they are analogously good, and that will be the form of the good.[16]

---

[15] For the view that Aristotle intends not just to list examples of goods in each category, but also to show what it is to be good in each category, see Ackrill (1972) and Irwin (1985, 302).

[16] Cf. Shields' Platonist who tries to escape Aristotle's arguments by concocting a higher-order account of goodness that will fit everything (Shields 1999, 208).

He might also object that Aristotle's earlier account of a long-lasting form rests on a misunderstanding of the abstract and timeless nature of the forms. However, Aristotle presumably thinks that if the Platonist makes any of these replies, he will have committed himself to a form of the good too abstract and general to be of any use. Hence his final arguments, making the case that even if there were such a form of the good, it would be useless for action. First, according to Aristotle, present-day craftsmen do not use or even seek the form of the good to help with their work. Second, the doctor is interested in particular cases, not universals. In fact, the physician is interested in the health of *this* human being.

Aristotle's final comments may appear particularly unfair to Plato. After all, in Plato's *Republic,* it is only the rulers who know the form of the good, not every individual. However, perhaps Aristotle could say that if the form of the good is supposed to relate to everything good, Plato is committed to its relevance for shoemaking and other crafts too.[17]

While Aristotle here clearly rejects Plato's form of the good, and the mathematical view of ethics that accompanies it, the broader implications of the argument are controversial. Suffice it to say that at least four clear points emerge from Aristotle's discussion of Plato. First, the good must be something practical, within our ken and power. Aristotle later emphasizes the practical nature of ethical thinking. Second, whereas Plato is sensitive to the similarities between different things, Aristotle is more sensitive to the differences between objects and the concreteness of particular things. This sensitivity is nowhere more evident than in his doctrine of the mean. Third, Aristotle thinks that things may be good by analogy. Analogies play an important role in Aristotle's own arguments in the *Nicomachean Ethics*, especially analogies with medicine and dietetics.[18] Fourth, to understand whether x is good, we need to know what kind of thing x is. This last point is crucial for Aristotle's argument from the human function. There, though, he adapts a Socratic argument from the first book of Plato's *Republic* that does not depend on Plato's forms.

1.2 The Teleological Approach

Chapters 1–2 and 7 in *Nicomachean Ethics* I present the teleological approach. The validity of the arguments here have been challenged, but

---

[17] Penner (1987, 40–41) cites Plato's *Cratylus* in arguing that on Plato's view, *knowledge* of the tools of one's craft *does* ultimately depend on knowledge of the Form of the good. General responses to Aristotle on Plato's behalf are beyond the scope of this Element, but see Santas (1989) and Yount (1998).

[18] On these, see Jaeger (1957) and Lloyd (1968).

the main point is that Aristotle is presenting a picture of how things are organized in the polis, with goods/goals and activities arranged in a hierarchy with the best good, the final *telos*, happiness, at the top. For example, the activity of bridle-making produces bridles used by the cavalry whose horsemanship and activities fall under generalship, which along with economics and rhetoric fall under the art of politics, which has as its aim the best good. Aristotle goes on to assume that if our own desires are structured in the same way, then if there is something that we wish for its own sake and not for the sake of anything else, that will be the best good.

In chapter 7, Aristotle distinguishes three kinds of goods/goals: those that are choiceworthy only for the sake of other things, for example, wealth, flutes, and instruments in general; those that are choiceworthy for their own sake and for the sake of happiness, for example, honor, pleasure, understanding, and every virtue; and those that are always chosen for their own sake and never for the sake of anything else, whose only member is happiness (*EN* I 7 1097a25-1097b6). The second category is controversial. Aristotle says that we would choose each of those goods even if it had no further result, but we also choose them for the sake of happiness.[19]

Here Aristotle is trying to establish that happiness is the final goal. He presents another argument for this conclusion from self-sufficiency. Aristotle rejects the view that someone living alone, independent of other human beings, is self-sufficient. Instead, what is self-sufficient is what suffices for someone in the context of family, friends, and society (*EN* I 7 1097b8-11). To put it simply, in order to be self-sufficient, we need other people. This fact is clearest in infancy, but it remains so in adulthood. A truly rugged individualist would not be self-sufficient or lead a happy life. According to Aristotle, happiness is self-sufficient because it makes a life choiceworthy and lacking nothing, and it makes a life choiceworthy because it is the most choiceworthy good.

The argument for this conclusion, which I shall call "the counting argument," contains an interesting grammatical construction in italics next.[20]

> We think it <happiness> is most choiceworthy, *not being counted together with <other goods>*, <for> counted together with <other goods>, it is clear that it is/would be more choiceworthy with the <addition of the> least of goods. (EN I 7 1097b16-18)

---

[19] See Gottlieb (2009, 134–150; 2021, 138–139).

[20] Compare the beginning of the second amendment of the US Constitution: "*A well-regulated militia being necessary to the security of a free state*, the right of the people to keep and bear arms shall not be infringed" (my emphasis).

The italicized construction could mean "since it is not counted together with <other goods>" or "when it is not counted together with <other goods>." For example, Irwin (2019) has "since," and Reeve (2014) has "when." Those accepting the first reading think that happiness must include all goods already. That is why one cannot add any other goods to it. Those accepting the second reading think that happiness is just the activity of contemplation. Other goods can be added to it, but when it is not counted together with those other goods, it is the most choiceworthy good.

There are problems with each reading. On the first, types of goods must be at issue, as it is implausible that happiness should include all token goods, but then it is puzzling what Aristotle means by the addition of the least of goods. On the second reading, there can be something more choiceworthy than happiness, namely, happiness plus other goods, and that seems to contradict the idea that happiness is the ultimate goal. My suggestion is that happiness cannot be counted together with other goods, because happiness is more like our notion of "quality of life" and not a quantitative notion at all. In *Categories* 14, Aristotle illustrates the distinction between a change in quantity and a change in quality with the example of a square that can increase in size with the addition of a gnomon, but will remain a square. (Here the gnomon is the L-shaped area that makes the difference between, say, a square with a 2-foot base and one with a 3-foot base.) If happiness is like a square, the addition of the least of goods (assuming, with Aristotle here, that it does not mar the symmetry) is like the addition of a gnomon. This interpretation has an important consequence. If Aristotle does not consider happiness a quantity, then it also makes no sense to speak of "maximizing happiness" on his view.[21]

1.3 The Biological and Psychological Approach

Aristotle then presents his third approach to happiness, the approach from a biological and psychological perspective. The argument has come to be known as the "function argument." Briefly, Aristotle argues that what counts as doing well for something, for example, an artisan, a musician, or a part of the body, depends on what it does, its function (*ergon*). So if human beings have a characteristic function, distinguishing them from other animals, and plants, doing well for a human being will depend on that. Aristotle argues that the characteristic function of humans has to do with the part of the human psyche that thinks and also desires and feels in response to thought, and so doing well for human beings, or happiness, must be carrying out the function of that part of the psyche well. Aristotle describes the parts of the human psyche in more detail

---

[21] This argument is derived from Gottlieb (2001a).

in the last chapter of the book, in preparation for his account of virtues of character.[22]

1.4 The Method of *Endoxa* Again

Applying the method of *endoxa*, Aristotle continues by arguing that his sketch of the good also harmonizes with what people think (*EN* I 8): The best kinds of good belong to the psyche.[23] They are not external goods, but external goods are required for happiness. Aristotle notes that his view is consistent with those who think happiness is virtue, or thoughtfulness (*phronēsis*), or some sort of wisdom, or pleasure. If so, the conclusion of the function argument must have been indeterminate enough to accommodate all these views. However, Aristotle says that pleasure comes from loving virtuous actions, not the type of gratification that he mentioned as one of the three ways of life he discussed earlier, and that the inscription at Delos (birthplace of Apollo) which says that what is most just is what is most beautiful, that being healthy is most beneficial, and that what is most pleasant is to get what one loves, is wrong in not recognizing that it is happiness that is best, most beautiful, and most pleasant. These are all stark reminders that the method of *endoxa* is not a method of deduction from what people think.

In fact, the method best aligns with Aristotle's earlier discussion in *Nicomachean Ethics* I 4, where he describes Plato's puzzlement about whether arguments go from origins or to origins, just as on a racecourse one may go from the starting line to the end and also back again. Aristotle says that we should begin with what is familiar to us, not what is known without qualification. I take it that Aristotle thinks that we should start with what is familiar to us, move on to what is known without qualification, and then return to what is familiar to us now seen in a new light. We were clued in to the origins all the time, but through a glass darkly. Aristotle's teleological and function arguments clarify what is right and what is wrong in people's ideas. We have run the racecourse to the end and are back where we started, with the original views clarified and revised.

1.4.1 Solon, Luck, and External Goods

Next Aristotle examines Solon's view about luck in *EN* I 10–11. According to Herodotus, Solon claimed that "a human being is entirely chance," depending

---

[22] On the function argument, see Gottlieb (2001a; 2009, 66–70; 2021, 18–20). The secondary literature is growing exponentially; see the bibliographies attached to these discussions, Rorty (1980) and Kraut (2006).

[23] Kraut (2018) takes this as the starting point for his revised account of Aristotle, where the goods of the soul are experiential in nature.

on what Aristotle would call external goods (goods outside the psyche), and that therefore one should not call anyone happy until that person is dead (Herodotus *Histories* I 30–33). Solon's comment combines two claims: first, one should not call a person happy before that person is dead; and second, one *can* call someone happy once that person is dead.

Aristotle reasonably points out that Solon cannot mean that someone could *be* happy after that person is dead, which would be absurd.[24] Therefore, argues Aristotle, Solon must mean that the person in question is now beyond good and bad fortune. But that, says Aristotle, is debatable: Since things can be good or bad for a person even if that person is not aware of them, they must also be so for a dead person, even if that person is not aware of them. As examples of good and bad things, Aristotle gives honors and dishonors, and successes and misfortunes of children and other descendants. (A modern parallel may be the "legacies" that politicians become concerned about when they are about to leave, or have left, office.) This raises a further problem, because if someone becomes happy or unhappy whenever there is a change in the fortunes of his children, for example, the happy person will be as changeable as a chameleon. In effect, Aristotle is posing a problem for Solon. If the fluctuations in fortune are so great that we cannot safely call someone happy during his or her lifetime, why aren't they equally great after death so that we should never call anyone happy?

Aristotle does not want to answer this question by rejecting an objective account of happiness and assuming that only perceived changes in our experience affect our happiness. An alternative account is therefore needed.

Aristotle argues that Solon's understanding of happiness is wrong because happiness does not depend solely on good or bad fortune concerning external goods. Although human beings need external goods for a happy life, "it is the activities in accordance with virtue that govern happiness (are *kuriai* of happiness) and the contrary activities that govern its contrary" (*EN* I 10 1100b9-11). In other words, we should not gauge a person's happiness simply by looking at the ups and downs in that person's fortunes, because these, unless very great, are not decisive. What *happens* to a person is less important than how the person deals with circumstances, through virtuous activity. The good person, he says, is not immune to bad luck, but will only be shaken from his happiness "by many great misfortunes, from which he will not become happy again in a short time, but if at all, in a long and complete one, by achieving many great and beautiful things" (*EN* I 11 1101a12-13). Therefore, according to Aristotle, it is reasonable to congratulate people on their happiness if they are virtuous, in anticipation of a continuing good life, and it is certainly possible to say whether they were

---

[24] Solon and Aristotle are therefore not assuming the existence of any afterlife.

happy once they are dead, when their happiness can no longer be decisively changed by fortunes or misfortunes.[25] Good people may become unhappy, but they will never become wretched (*athlioi*), because they will never do vicious actions. As Aristotle explains in the succeeding discussion of encomia, we praise people for being virtuous, but congratulate them for being happy, presumably because happiness is not completely in their control.

1.5 The Three Approaches in the *Eudemian Ethics*

Although the three approaches to happiness are still apparent in the *Eudemian Ethics* (*EE* I and II), Aristotle's discussion in the *Eudemian Ethics* is sometimes shorter than that of the *Nicomachean Ethics*, sometimes more expansive, and sometimes ordered very differently. For example, the *Eudemian Ethics* has only brief comments about Solon and encomia, and in the midst of its own function argument. Yet there is an important paragraph about luck early on where Aristotle comments that if living well is merely a matter of luck, or just by nature, it would be a hopeless aspiration for many (*EE* I 3 1215a12-14), and Aristotle has a discussion of a different type of luck, unparalleled in the *EN*, in *EE* VIII. In book I of the *Eudemian Ethics*, Aristotle has more expansive comments on the four lives, noting Anaxagoras's view that the person who is happy is a strange person, someone who leads a life painlessly and purely in relation to justice or who engages in divine contemplation (*EE* I 4 1215b11-14), explained as contemplating the heavens and the order of the whole universe (*EE* I 5 1216a13-14). Aristotle also suggests that there may be other pleasures that contribute to the happy life as well as some kinds of physical gratification (*EE* I 5 1216a30-37), looking forward to his discussion of pleasure in the common books.

The *Eudemian Ethics* also contains a discussion of the things that would make life not worth living, for example, disease, extreme pain, storms, and pleasure of an ugly kind (*EE* I 5 1215b19-26). There is no parallel to this passage in the *Nicomachean Ethics*.

The *Eudemian* discussion of Plato's form of the good contains a longer section against the idea of a common good, and ends with the conclusion that the good must be the ultimate goal of human action. Although the *Eudemian Ethics* does not begin with the *Nicomachean* hierarchy of goals, the hierarchy of sciences appears instead toward the end of his criticism of Plato. The *Eudemian Ethics* also has a prologue to the function argument where

---

[25] It is controversial what Aristotle's conclusion is, because he uses rhetorical questions (*EN* I 10 1101a14-16). However, his final, nonrhetorical comment that the blessed, that is, happy individual is the person who has and will keep the goods he has, supports my interpretation of the role of virtue (*EN* I 10 1101a16-20). I assume that "blessed" and "happy" are interchangeable here.

Aristotle distinguishes different types of function. For example, the function of a shoemaker is a shoe, not shoemaking, whereas the function of sight is seeing. (Here "function" is a less felicitous translation of *"ergon"* than "work," but the Greek term is the same.[26]) There is a hierarchy of dispositions and activities. Here the importance of activity is argued for, rather than just assumed, as it is in the *Nicomachean* function argument.

As for the method of *endoxa*, Aristotle adds that we can discount the views of children and the insane. While in chapter 3 he says that we do not need to examine the views of the hoi polloi, in chapter 6 he more charitably says that "each person has something of their own to contribute to the truth and that, . . . starting with things that are correctly said, but not clearly, we should proceed to what is stated clearly, always changing what is more familiar to us, but expressed in a confused way, into what is stated clearly" (*EE* I 51216b30-35). Here the *Eudemian* discussion is more expansive than the *Nicomachean* discussion. Aristotle goes on to say that the *philosopher* needs to know *why* something is so as well as *that* it is so (what Aristotle calls "the why" and "the that"), but that uneducated people can often be misled by bad arguments. We should therefore pay more attention to what the conclusion is than to the argument for it. This also explains the *Nicomachean* obscure saying that if the that is sufficiently apparent, we do not need to know the why (*EN* I 4 1095b6-7).[27] In the *Eudemian Ethics*, Aristotle is also clear about what can and cannot be given a demonstrative (or deductive) argument. At the end of his discussion of Plato's form of the good, he notes that no one demonstrates that health or any other starting point is a good, unless that person is a sophist (*EE* I 8 1218b22-24).

The *Eudemian Ethics* begins with Aristotle's criticism of the inscription of Delos, showing straight off the bat how what is familiar to the Greeks may need revision.

Significantly, there is no counting argument in the *Eudemian Ethics*. As we shall see, that meshes with the fact that the *Nicomachean Ethics* emphasizes the nonquantitative aspects of Aristotle's theory more than does the *Eudemian Ethics*.[28]

Both preliminary *Nicomachean* and *Eudemian* discussions are openended. We do not yet know what the particular virtues are or how these may or may not be combined. Nor do we know precisely what kind of thinking and feeling is involved in exercising the rational part of the psyche

---

[26] For the translation "achievement," see Baker (2015).

[27] See Gottlieb (2001a; 2009, 182–185).

[28] Allan (1961) gave a classic argument for the mathematical presentation of the *Eudemian Ethics*. That is not the emphasis on mathematics I have in mind here.

to lead a happy life. The *Eudemian* discussion may be even more open-ended than the *Nicomachean* discussion, because the distinction between the lives of plants and animals is not made until after its version of the function argument has come to a close.

2 Virtue of Character and the Doctrine of the Mean

I begin with a few reflections on Aristotelian virtue of character. In both the *Eudemian* and *Nicomachean Ethics*, there are two types of virtue: virtue of character and virtue of thought. The latter is found in the part of the soul that has thought; the former in the part of the soul that is responsive to thought (*EN* I 13 1103a1-7, *EE* II 1 1220a5-12) – that is to say, the part of the soul that has desires, including feelings.[29]

As Aristotle argues in the *Eudemian Ethics*, although knowing what virtue is is a beautiful thing, we want to know how virtue arises, because we want to be virtuous as opposed to merely knowing what virtue is (*EE* I 5 1216b19-25).[30] In the *Nicomachean Ethics*, Aristotle puts the point more strongly, saying that the aim of his discussion is not to know what virtue is, but to become good, otherwise it would be of no use to us (*EN* II 2 1103b29-31).

In both works, Aristotle stresses that we are not born virtuous, but we become virtuous by habituation (*ethismōi*), or, more precisely, by practicing the right actions and cultivating the right feelings at the same time.[31] In the *Nicomachean Ethics*, Aristotle explains how we come to enjoy doing what we should, because enjoying doing what we should is a sign of good character (*EN* II 3). Having achieved a virtue, we are disposed to act and feel accordingly. Hence, virtue is a disposition (*hexis*), not a feeling, nor a mere capacity to feel. While the *Nicomachean Ethics* gives a long list of the feelings – "appetite, anger (*orgē*), fear, confidence, envy, joy, love, hate, longing, emulation and sympathy, and in general what is accompanied by pleasure or pain" (*EN* II 5 1105b21-23) – the *Eudemian Ethics* just mentions anger (*thumos*), fear, shame (not specifically mentioned in the *Nicomachean* list), and appetite, adding anything that is accompanied by perceptual pleasure and pain (*EE* II 2 1220b12-13). These feelings are occurrent.[32]

---

[29] For a contrary view, see Lorenz (2009b).

[30] I use the translation "beautiful" for "*kalon*." This translation emphasizes the aesthetic side to the *kalon* but is not intended to downplay the ethical side (Gottlieb 2021, 122–142). However, the translation is controversial. See, for example, Irwin (2011) as opposed to Kraut (2013).

[31] On the workings of habituation, including action, thought, desire, and feelings, see Gottlieb (2021, 42–52). See too Burnyeat (1980) and Kosman (1980) with Joachim (1951).

[32] For a detailed account of the feelings, see *Rhetoric* II 1–11 and Gottlieb (2021, 24–41).

In the *Nicomachean Ethics*, Aristotle explains the capacity to feel as follows:

> By capacities I mean what we have when we are said to be capable of these feelings, capable of being angry, for example, or of feeling pain, or of feeling sympathy (*EN* II 3 1105b23-25).

> [W]e are neither said to be good nor bad, nor are we praised or blamed, in virtue of simply being capable of feeling. Furthermore, while we are capable <of feeling> by nature, we do not become good or bad by nature.
>
> (*EN* II 5 1106a7-10)

In the *Eudemian Ethics*, however, the capacities Aristotle has in mind are more clearly matters of temperament. There he distinguishes capacities from feelings as follows:

> By "capacities" (*dunameis*) I mean those in relation to which people are described as actively experiencing feelings (*kata ta pathē hoi energountes*), for example, being irascible (*orgilos*), insensible (*analgētos*), erotic, prone to shame, and shameless. Dispositions are all those causes of these things (*tauta*) being either in accord with thought (*logos*) or the opposite, for example, bravery, temperance, cowardice, intemperance.
>
> (*EE* II 2 1220b15-20)

Kenny (2011) translates "*dunameis*" as "susceptibilities," Rackham (1981) translates "irascible" ("*orgilos*") as a temperament, "choleric," and Woods (1992) translates "insensible" ("*analgētos*") as "phlegmatic." Their translations support my interpretation.

If this interpretation is correct, then it is reasonable to suppose that what Aristotle goes on to discuss with the obscure terminology of "*mesotētes* ... pathētikai*" ("means involving feelings") in the classification of "*tōn pathēmatōn*" are matters of temperament too (*EN* III 7 1233b17-19; *EE* III 7 1234a25-26).[33] It is not possible for something that is merely a matter of temperament to be a virtue or vice strictly, fully, or properly (*kuriōs*). In the *Eudemian Ethics*, Aristotle considers three of the proper virtues in the *Nicomachean Ethics*, friendliness, truthfulness, and wit, to be merely a matter of temperament, or perhaps we might say, a matter of personality as opposed to character, contributing, or perhaps being ascribed to, the natural virtues (*EN* III 7 1234a25-28).[34] As Aristotle explains, each virtue occurs naturally and other-wise. In the second case, it involves thoughtfulness (*phronēsis*) (*EE* III 7 1234a26). Here, Aristotle refers to a later discussion in a common book

---

[33] It may or not be significant that he uses a different term from "*pathē*."

[34] Fortenbaugh (1968) dubbed these the "questionable mean-dispositions." I owe the translation "ascribed to" to Dalimier (2013).

where he distinguishes natural and full-blown virtue (*EN* VI/*EE* V 13 1144b1-17). I shall return to this point later.

Both the *Eudemian* and *Nicomachean Ethics* contain Aristotle's signature doctrine of the mean. In the *Nicomachean Ethics*, this combines three theses: (1) Each virtue is in a mean between two vices, one of excess and one of deficiency. (2) The virtuous person's character is balanced, that is, in equilibrium.[35] His character is in a mean (*en mesotēti*) in such a way that he hits the mean (*meson*), acting and feeling when he should, at things he should, in relation to the people he should, for the goal he should, and in the way he should.[36] (3) The mean is relative to us, depending on the agent's abilities and particular circumstances.[37]

While both treatises seem to accept each of these views, the introductory discussion in the *Eudemian Ethics* is very compressed. According to the *Eudemian Ethics*:

> [I]n every continuum that is divisible there is excess and deficiency and a mean (*meson*), and these either in relation to one another or in relation to us, for example, in gymnastics, medicine, house-building, navigation, and any type of action both scientific and non-scientific, technical and non-technical, for a process is continuous and action is a process. In all <these things> the mean in relation to ourselves is best, for this is as knowledge and thought (*logos*) prescribe. (*EE* II 3 1220b22-29)

The *Eudemian Ethics* also describes each virtue as a mean relating to continua of pleasures and pains, with the good person experiencing the right amount of pleasure and pain (*EE* II 5 1222a10-17).[38]

These remarks are obscure. Aristotle clarifies them in the *Nicomachean Ethics*. First he notes:

> In every continuum that is divisible we can take more, less, and equal, and each of them either in the object itself or relative to us. The equal is some mean (*meson*) between excess and deficiency. By the mean in the object I mean what is equidistant from each extreme which is one and the same for

---

[35] This interpretation goes back at least as far as Grant (1874).

[36] Young (1996) refers to the fact that each virtue is between two vices as its "location" as opposed to intermediacy, which is aiming at the intermediate on a particular occasion. One might think that Aristotle's distinction between "*mesotēs*" (mean) and "*meson*" lines up with this distinction, but it does not. Aristotle uses "*mesos*" indiscriminately. See *EN* II 8 1109a7 and 1109a17. Even Irwin (2019) translates "*mesos*" there as "intermediate condition."

[37] For a defense of this view, contra Brown (1997; 2014), see Gottlieb (2009, 19–37). The distinction drawn in the previous footnote is independent of my disagreement with Brown about whether relativity includes relativity to the agent's particular abilities. My discussion of relativity in Gottlieb (2009) elaborates the issues raised by Brown and ends up with a complicated picture that I have simplified here.

[38] Given the compressed nature of Aristotle's style, Kenny (2011) and Inwood and Woolf (2013)'s translations differ. Kenny (2011) concludes: "The good man, however, has the feelings he ought to have." Inwood and Woolf (2013) conclude: "But the good person acts as one ought."

all. But relative to us is what is neither excessive nor deficient. This is not one,
nor the same for all. (*EN* II 6 1106a26-33)

Aristotle then clarifies "the mean relative to us" by distinguishing the mean in
the object and the mean relative to us (*EN* II 6 1106a26-1106b3), using the
example of Milo, the six-time champion wrestler at the Olympic Games, versus
the beginning athlete. If ten pounds of food is too much and two too little, six
would be the arithmetic mean, but what Milo and the beginner need is the mean
relative to each. What is a suitable amount of food for Milo (who was reputed to
have eaten a whole joint of beef at one sitting) is not what is suitable for the
beginner. While Aristotle rejects a one-size-fits-all approach, the mean relative
to us is not relativist, depending solely on what the agent thinks, but is an
objective matter.

The analogy with Milo helps us to understand the murkier view presented in
the *Eudemian Ethics*. Aristotle stresses that the mean is not arithmetical, which
matches his comment in the *Nicomachean*, though not in the *Eudemian Ethics*,
that we should only expect claims in ethics to be "for the most part" (*EN* I 3
1094b21).

Aristotle's discussion in *Nicomachean Ethics* II is more expansive than that
in *Eudemian Ethics* II. He uses an analogy with skills (which he calls
"*epistēmai*," sciences, since he has yet to draw the distinction made in *EE* V/
EN VI) to argue that when a product is well made, we say that nothing can be
added or taken away; deficiency and excess destroy its being good (literally,
"the well" (*to eu*), but the mean preserves it (*EN* II 6 1106b8-12). It is hard to hit
the mean directly, for example giving and spending money to whom one ought,
when one ought, and so forth. Aristotle says that for this reason, doing so is rare
and praiseworthy and beautiful (*kalon*). Here the beautiful is connected with
hitting the mean. A second best way of hitting the mean in ethics is to avoid the
extremes to which one is prey, and to avoid pleasure. This advice is oversimpli-
fied at this juncture. As we shall see, not all pleasure is to be avoided. These
points are not made in *Eudemian Ethics* II.[39]

More about the doctrine of the mean can be gleaned from examining the
particular virtues of character and temperamental means, as in the following
section.

In both treatises, Aristotle stresses that the virtuous mean is given by thought
(*EE* III 1220b28), and in the *Nicomachean Ethics* he explains what virtue of

---

[39] It is no objection to the doctrine of the mean that some actions or feelings like murder or spite are
always bad. Murder is killing in the way one should not at the time one should not and so forth,
and spite is feeling joy in the way one should not and so forth. As Aristotle says, to think
differently is like thinking that there can be a mean of a cowardly or intemperate action (*EN* II 6
1107a9-21).

character is as follows: "Virtue of character is a prohairetic disposition, being in a mean relative to us, defined by the thought (*logos*), i.e., by the thought by which the person with thoughtfulness (*ho phronimos*) would define it" (*EN* II 6 1106b36-1107a2).[40] In the *Nicomachean Ethics*, Aristotle says that virtues are not identical with feelings because one can have a feeling without choice (*prohairesis*). In the *Eudemian Ethics*, the difference between being a temperamental mean and being a proper virtue is that the former does not involve choice. While we have to wait until *EE* V/*EN* VI for thoughtfulness and the other virtues of thought to be fully explained, the next topics in both works are the voluntary and choice, for all chosen actions are voluntary but not vice versa, and good choice is required for virtue.

Nicomachean Ethics II provides a preview of the importance of choice, which Aristotle introduces by way of an independently interesting puzzle about becoming good, not provided in the *Eudemian Ethics*. How can we become just by doing just actions, for example, if we are not already just? Surely, we need to be just already to do just actions, just as we need to be literate or musicians to do musical or literate actions. The puzzle has a similar structure to the famous paradox of inquiry: If one already knows something, there is no point in seeking knowledge of it, and if one does not know it, one will be unable to start the search (cf. Plato's *Meno* 80E). Here, if one is already doing just and temperate actions, one must already be just and temperate and so will not need to become so. Presumably, if one is not already doing just and temperate actions, one will not be just and temperate and will be unable to become so.

Aristotle explains that even in the case of a skill, for example, literacy, one can spell correctly by chance or by following someone else's instructions. But to be literate, one must spell in a literate way, in accordance with the knowledge of spelling in us.

According to Aristotle, the ethical case is more complicated. While one can assess the product of a skill on its own, however it was made, ethical actions must be done justly or temperately. One must (1) know what one is doing, (2) choose the actions for their own sake, and (3) do them stably and unchangingly. Choice is important. The point seems to be that while one can assess the product of, say, shoemaking, the shoe, independently of knowing how it was made, one cannot do this with the "product" of virtue, ethical action. One can see whether the shoe does its job for walking, independent of the motives of the shoemaker, but one cannot do this in the same way with, for example, a generous action. While one can see an agent give some money to someone else, one cannot tell

---

[40] An alternate manuscript has "in the way in which the person with thoughtfulness."

from this mere behavior whether this was a generous action or an unjust bribe. One needs to know the character and motives of the agent.

Here, Aristotle is underestimating the role of an artisan in the evaluation of the product of a skill. For example, an exact replica of a painting by Van Gogh would not be evaluated in the same way as one made by the artist himself. While Aristotle seems to assume that a product made by chance can be evaluated in the same way as one created by skill – a word can be spelled correctly either way – one may wonder whether a word spelled correctly by chance counts as a word at all, rather than just a string of squiggles, just as lucky behavior does not count as a generous or brave action.

Since just and temperate actions must be done justly and temperately, and young children do not have choice, as Aristotle explains in the next book, it may seem as if Aristotle has not solved the puzzle. As in my example of Aristotelian generosity, we need to distinguish the mere behavior of the learner from the full-blown action of the good person. Hitting the mean (where this is the intermediate) involves feeling and acting as when one should and so forth *and in the way one should*. While one may be able to hit the other parameters of the mean while a learner, one cannot do so *in the way one should*, that is, virtuously, unless one is a good person. However, there is no quantum leap toward becoming a good person. It is a gradual process where thought and feeling develop together.[41]

3 The Voluntary and Choice

In both the *Nicomachean* and *Eudemian Ethics,* virtue of character involves choice, and actions that are chosen are a subset of those that are voluntary. The voluntary is therefore the obvious topic to be discussed next in each of these works.[42]

3.1 The Voluntary

Aristotle's discussion of the voluntary in *Nicomachean Ethics* III 1 begins with the following comments: "Virtue, then, is about feelings and actions.[43] They receive praise or blame if they are voluntary but sympathetic consideration (*suggnōmē*), sometimes even sympathy (*eleos*), if they are involuntary"

---

[41] On this interpretation, Aristotle need not be losing sight of his "central insight that the acquisition of skills is cumulative" (Taylor 2006, 82).

[42] Opinions differ as to the relative merits of the *Eudemian* and *Nicomachean* account. Kenny (1979) thinks that the *Eudemian* account is superior. Charles (2012) demurs. For an excellent discussion about why "voluntary" is the best translation of "*to hekousion,*" see Meyer (2012, 9–14).

[43] Aspasius thinks that the voluntary applies only to actions.

(*EN* III 1 1109b30-32).[44] Presumably it is bad involuntary actions that receive sympathetic consideration. Unlike modern forgiveness, Aristotelian sympathetic consideration does not extend to those who have acted badly voluntarily.[45] On Aristotle's account, bad involuntary actions receive sympathetic consideration if they are caused merely by external force, where the origin is not in the agent (a strict criterion according to which in this case they may not count as actions at all), or if they are done due to ignorance of the relevant particulars in cases where the agent also regrets the action. If one does not regret a bad action done due to ignorance of the relevant particulars, the action counts as nonvoluntary, one possible reason being that sympathetic consideration would hardly be appropriate in such a case. Also, not knowing what is virtuous in general is not exculpatory.

The category of the nonvoluntary does not appear in the *Eudemian Ethics*. Nor does sympathetic consideration have the prominence that it does in the *Nicomachean Ethics*.

In his *Nicomachean Ethics*, Aristotle explains that "mixed actions," actions under duress, while involuntary other things being equal (literally, without qualification, *haplōs*), are voluntary in the very context in which they performed. For example, throwing cargo overboard is involuntary, other things being equal, but not when done to save the lives of passengers and crew in a storm.[46] (We would blame someone who did not throw the cargo overboard in a storm.) There is one proviso, and here too sympathetic consideration plays a role. In the *Nicomachean Ethics*, Aristotle argues that sympathetic consideration applies to things that overstrain human nature: "In some cases there is not praise, but sympathetic consideration when someone does things he should not because of such things that overstrain human nature and that no one would withstand" (*EN* III 1 1110a23-26). The things that overstrain human nature here appear to be external factors. Aristotle says that the things that caused Euripides's Alcmaeon to kill his mother (namely, his father's curse) did not overstrain human nature.

True, Aristotle mentions sympathetic consideration in cases of overstraining human nature in the *Eudemian Ethics*, but it is unclear whether he accepts the particular examples he is reporting, which are examples of constraining internal as opposed to external factors:

---

[44] The translation "sympathetic consideration," following the etymology of "*sug-gnōmē*" consideration with, is by Broadie and Rowe (2002) and Reeve (2014).

[45] Sachs (2001) and Curzer (2012) translate "*suggnōmē*" as "forgiveness."

[46] Aristotle's other example of helping a tyrant do something ugly to save the lives of one's family is more difficult. On mixed actions, including the case of the cargo, and modern moral dilemmas, see Gottlieb (2009, 115–133). On evaluating actions in gray zones, situations where the oppressed help their oppressors, see Card (2002, 211–235).

> Hence many regard even love (*erōta*) as involuntary, and certain cases of anger and certain natural <conditions> as being too strong for nature, and we have sympathetic consideration on the grounds that they are of such a nature as to force nature. (*EE* II 8 1225a21-22)

In the *Nicomachean Ethics*, Aristotle memorably says that it is hard to know what to do at the price of what (*EN* III 1110a29-30). In both works, the stakes are important, and so is the context.

The discussion of the voluntary is arranged very differently in the *Eudemian Ethics*. Instead of starting the discussion by mentioning reactive attitudes, Aristotle starts in a very general way by explaining that all substances are naturally origins (*archai*) of a sort. For example, humans beget humans. However, only a human being is an origin of certain actions, While if (contrary to the axioms of geometry) a triangle contained three right angles, a quadrilateral would have six, and so forth, mathematical origins are not *controlling* origins (*kuriai archai*) because they are not origins of change. (The mathematical example is interesting because it shows up again in a common book.) Humans are origins and are in control of what is up to them.

One might expect the text to proceed along *Nicomachean* lines, explaining how, if an action is voluntary, the origin of that action must be in the agent. Instead, we get a series of logic-chopping arguments to show that the voluntary is not identical with desire (*orexis*) or choice (*prohairesis*) and therefore must be in accord with thought (*dianoia*). Aristotle divides desire into wish (*boulēsis*), anger (*thumos*), and appetite (*epithumia*), rejecting each of these possibilities in turn. Since he has shown that the voluntary is not the same as what is wished, and choice is narrower than wish, he will also have shown that the voluntary is not the same as choice.[47]

A main part of the discussion relies on the assumption that the involuntary is what is done under constraint (*biai*) and is painful.[48] Aristotle also makes the point not made elsewhere that thought may be involuntary as well, for example, prophesying. This belies a common modern view that thought is always under our control, and only feelings get out of control. As in the *Nicomachean Ethics*, Aristotle discusses what the stakes have to be for actions to be involuntary. Here he argues that the action is voluntary if the agent chooses the goal although not the specific thing that she does. Presumably, then, in a storm one chooses safety, but not throwing the cargo overboard. Yet throwing the cargo overboard to save the passengers and crew is voluntary. This is a different analysis from the

---

[47] Here I follow Rowe's notes at *EE* II 8 1223b39 (Rowe forthcoming).
[48] See Susan Sauvé Meyer (2012, 76–78, 83–84).

Nicomachean version, although the conclusion that the action is voluntary is the same.

The argument also contains a discussion of *akrasia* and *enkrateia*, cases where the agent has an appetite (or anger) that is contrary to what she wishes and believes best. If she acts on that feeling, she is akratic, if not, she is enkratic. (This conflict model of *akrasia* can also be found in *Nicomachean Ethics* I 13.) One important point stands out. Although each part of the soul seems to be forced by the other, "the whole soul acts voluntarily, in the case of the akratic and enkratic, and neither is forced, because we have both <appetite and reason> by nature" (*EE* II 8 1224b27-28). The idea that the whole soul initiates action, and not just the rational part, combined with the view that a human being is the origin of action, is a pivotal point in the common book *EE* V/*EN* VI. *Akrasia* is discussed at length in the common book *EE* VI/*EN* VII.

Aristotle's discussion also contains his thoughts on natural processes like aging. He concludes with a definition of the voluntary that mentions all the relevant particulars that one should know, and not incidentally. His final discussion about thought is important in drawing distinctions between different kinds of knowledge that are crucial for his defense of *akrasia* in common book *EE* VI/*EN* VII 3.[49]

3.2 Choice

In both the *Nicomachean* and *Eudemian Ethics*, Aristotle considers whether choice is appetite, spirit (*thumos*), wish, or belief, perhaps options that someone familiar with Plato's division of the soul into the reasoning, spirited, and appetitive parts would take.[50] Aristotle argues that it is identical with none of these, although he leaves open that it might be a combination.[51] On a positive note, he argues that deliberation is involved in choice, and explains what deliberation is about.[52] In the *Nicomachean Ethics,* he points out that one does not deliberate about eternal things. In the *Eudemian Ethics*, too, he says that we do not deliberate about things such as that the diagonal of the square is incommensurable with its side (*EE* II 10 1226a3). Such comments can be seen as precursors to the distinction between the different objects of the theoretical and practical parts of the soul as discussed in the common book *EE* V/*EN* VI.

---

[49] See the end of this section for Aristotle's thoughts on whether the dispositions of virtue and vice are voluntary.

[50] On Plato's moral psychology, see Meinwald (2016) and Kamtekar (2017, 152–154).

[51] See Gottlieb (2021) for such an interpretation of the *Nicomachean Ethics* and common book *EE* V/*EN VI* on choice.

[52] For more on deliberation, see Wiggins (1975–1976) and McDowell (2009, 41–58).

In both works, Aristotle says that we do not deliberate about goals. According to the *Nicomachean Ethics*, the physician does not deliberate about whether to cure. Presumably, this means that when confronted with a patient, the physician does not reconsider his career in medicine, but what to do to restore the patient to health (*EN* III 3 1112b12-13).

Deliberation is not sufficient for choice. Choice is deliberative desire. (Aristotle elaborates this point further in the common book *EE* V/*EN* VI.) In the *Eudemian Ethics*, Aristotle says that choice is neither belief nor desire, but belief plus desire when these follow from deliberation (*EE* II 10 1227a3-5). The discussion in *Nicomachean Ethics* says that when we have deliberated, we desire to do the action in accordance with our wish (*EN* III 3 1113a11-12).[53] This leaves open the view that wish, the motivation for the goal, as described in the next section, is channeled into the motivation for the action. I have argued that motivation from feelings is included as well. The desire does not just spring up at the end of deliberation, as might seem the case from the *Eudemian* discussion.[54]

On the *Eudemian* discussion, Kenny argues:

> It is obvious that it is a very solemn kind of choice, made after deliberation, and on the basis of a thought-out plan of life. Carrying out a monastic vow, or New Year's resolution seems to be the closest thing in modern life to making an Aristotelian choice. Perhaps 'resolution' would be a more appropriate translation, or perhaps one should write 'Choice' with a capital C.
>
> (Kenny 2011, 159)

Leaving aside the un-Aristotelian examples, this is far too narrow. Even in the *Eudemian Ethics*, Aristotle gives the example of a person going for a walk to fetch his belongings (*EE* II 10 1226b28-29).

In the following chapter of the *Eudemian Ethics,* Aristotle comes to the provocative conclusion that virtue makes the goal (*skopos*) correct, not what contributes to the goal (*ta pros ton skopon*) (*EE* II 11 1227b23-24). In brief, Aristotle's argument for this conclusion is that just as in the theoretical sciences (*tais theōrētikais*), the starting points are hypotheses, so in the productive sciences (*tais poiētikais*) the starting point is the goal. In ethical reasoning, this goal is arrived at either by correct thought (*orthos logos*), here equated with deductive reasoning, or it is given by virtue. Since it cannot be arrived at by deductive reasoning, it must be given by virtue.

---

[53] Here, following Irwin (2019), I read "wish" instead of "deliberation" where the manuscripts differ.

[54] On desire not springing up at the end of deliberation, see Pearson (2012, 184–185).

The argument is fallacious. Although the starting points of the theoretical disciplines are not reached by deduction (for then they would not be starting points), according to Aristotle's *Analytics* (which he just cited at *EE* II 10 1227a10), understanding (*nous*) provides the starting points, and there is no reason why an analogue to that type of understanding should not be included in a broader notion of correct thought. Even if understanding is reached by ethical habituation, that itself would include developing both feelings and careful thought in order to hit the mean. As Ackrill (1973, 29) puts it, "thought and desire seem to be involved with one another at each stage of effective deliberation and action."

When Aristotle repeats the claim in a common book that virtue makes the goal correct, he also notes that thoughtfulness (*phronēsis*), there equated with correct thought, does so too (*EE/EN* VI 9 1142b31-33). This is possible since Aristotle there sees that one cannot have virtue of character proper without thoughtfulness and conversely, and that virtue is an integral part of the practical syllogism. (Aristotle there takes the analogy between theoretical and practical thinking a step further than he does in the *Eudemian* discussion.)

In the *Nicomachean Ethics*, the discussion about choice is followed by a puzzle about wish, which is solved by disagreeing with Socrates that everyone, and not just the good person, wishes for what is really good (*EN* III 4). Here Aristotle introduces his view of the good person as the standard and measure (*kanōn kai metron*), a view only presented in these terms in the *Nicomachean Ethics*. I shall return to this doctrine in my discussion of pleasure later on.

Next Aristotle addresses the question whether virtue and vice are voluntary (*EN* III 5). This question is not raised in the *Eudemian Ethics*. The answer is "yes": "We are in a way co-causes of our dispositions (*kai gar tōn hexeōn sunaitioi pōs autoi esmen*)" (*EN* III 5 1114b22-23). How Aristotle arrives at this answer and what it means is unclear.[55] But, as we shall see, the question arises again when Aristotle discusses particular virtues in his *Nicomachean Ethics*, though not in the *Eudemian Ethics*.

4 Virtues of Character and Temperamental Means

In the *Nicomachean Ethics*, the list of virtues of character contains five named and five nameless virtues, as well as justice, the topic of the first common book. It also includes two temperamental means that also appear in the *Eudemian Ethics*. In the *Eudemian Ethics*, no virtues are called nameless, and four of the five *Nicomachean* nameless virtues do not count as proper virtues. For ease of

---

[55] For a fuller discussion, see Gottlieb (2021, 56–61) with Meyer (2012, 122–148). On the mutability of different types of character in Aristotle, see Anton (2014).

exposition, I shall discuss the virtues of character in the order that they appear in the *Nicomachean Ethics*, pausing to include the *Eudemian* temperamental mean of dignity, and ending with discussion of some temperamental means that are not virtues in either work.

It is customary to say that the different virtues cover different areas of life, which is true, but that does not tell us what the virtues are. In other ethical systems, what Aristotle calls excess vices or deficient vices count as the virtues. It is the doctrine of the mean that is crucial in telling us what the virtues of character are. Moreover, Aristotle never claims that his list of the virtues is exhaustive. We may find other virtues of character that are Aristotelian means as well.[56]

4.1 Bravery

The virtue of bravery comes first in Aristotle's discussion of the particular virtues of character in both the *Eudemian* and *Nicomachean Ethics*, probably because it was the most familiar to his Greek audience. Young men were brought up reading the works of Homer with the reverence shown to the bible. In the works of Homer, the men went out to fight in war and the women stayed at home, so bravery was the quintessential virtue. Just as the Greek term "*aretē*," like the English term "virtue," literally refers to the quality of a man ("*anēr*" in Greek and "*vir*" in Latin), the Greek term "*andreia*" for bravery, or courage, literally means "manliness." As we shall see, Aristotle makes the striking point that Homeric bravery does not count as true bravery, and he includes many other virtues, especially nameless ones, that go beyond conventional views.

In each work, Aristotle maintains that bravery comes between the vice of deficiency, cowardice, and the vice of excess, rashness. The brave are disposed to have fear and confidence when they ought, as they ought, and so forth.

In the *Eudemian Ethics*, Aristotle is concerned to explain what fearful things the brave person fears, whether things that frighten just him, or things that frighten human beings generally. The discussion is quite convoluted, as Aristotle tries to explain which is correct, and in what respect the brave person is fearless and in what respect he is not, without mentioning confidence. He also has a discussion of the difference between enduring heat and cold and enduring life-threatening pain. In the *Nicomachean Ethics*, Aristotle takes a different tack, giving concrete examples of things that humans fear: bad reputation,

---

[56] For a detailed discussion of how Aristotle arrives at his list of virtues, and on candidates for the virtues, ancient and modern, see Gottlieb (2009, 74–91). On the fact that we do not start off with an outline of the happy life and then find the virtues in it, see the conclusion to this Element.

poverty, sickness, lack of friends, and death (*EN* III 6 1115a10-11). He argues that death is the most frightening thing, and that the fully brave person is concerned with the most beautiful death, that in war. Those who fear poverty, sickness, and the like are brave only by similarity (*EN* III 6 1115a19). In the *Eudemian Ethics*, Aristotle also says that the brave person acts for the sake of the beautiful, but since he does not provide the *Nicomachean* examples, he does not explicitly say that death in war is the primary case. If the purview of bravery is different in the two texts, the *Eudemian* may be harking back to the Socratic view that bravery is a broad virtue, perhaps better translated there as "courage," the preferred translation of Kenny (2011).

Aristotle's discussion raises the question whether bravery best involves risking a beautiful death in war. Aristotle says that it is right and even beautiful to fear bad reputation, but that this is the decent rather than the brave thing to do. We should not fear poverty and sickness, if these were not caused by ourselves, he says. However, he points out, no one receives medals for dealing with poverty and sickness, as do the brave in battle, a sign that the latter are the most beautiful deaths. Certainly, we do not choose to be in dire situations at sea or in sickness, whereas people do choose to face the dangers of war. For the ancient Greeks, there was probably not much to be done if one was ill (physicians would simply state the critical days where one would die or survive the illness) and so not much choice if one was ill. As Aristotle argues in both works, virtue involves choice. In modern times, we need not be so passive in the face of illness. We may also wonder why Aristotle does not consider the case of physicians being brave, if they treat those with fatal contagious diseases.

Both the *Nicomachean* and *Eudemian Ethics* mention the "rash coward." In the *Eudemian Ethics*, such a person is mentioned briefly in discussing the mean: "Sometimes the very same people are rash cowards or are wasteful in some things and stingy in others" (*EE* III 7 1234b2-3). In the *Nicomachean Ethics*, this person is discussed in the context of bravery. Such a person talks a good game before the battle about what he is going to do, but then runs away. He is overconfident before the battle, but then too fearful. The example poses a problem for a certain way of understanding the mean. If there is one continuum of fear, for example, and the deficiency and excess lie at opposite extremes, having two continua means that we have two excesses and deficiencies, and can therefore concoct extra vices, violating the triadic schema. In the case of bravery, some philosophers have suggested that there should also be two means here, and not just one (discussed in the classic paper by Pears [1980]). The problem is not confined to the case of bravery. Other vices that have two continua, for example, generosity, which concerns both giving and taking, have the same problem. In fact, all the virtues have multiple continua, given that we should do the right thing, at the right time, in the right way, and so forth. If that is the case, perhaps we should rethink a quantitative view of the mean. We also need to consider why Aristotle presents a system of triads, if there are many more vices than just two per virtue of character. I shall consider that question when we come to the virtue of magnanimity.

Both works contain a discussion of five conditions that resemble bravery but are not. The point of the discussion is to show that the brave person must be motivated by the beautiful (*to kalon*), and not simply by shame (like the Homeric heroes) or coercion (citizen "bravery"), experience about protecting oneself from dangers (military "bravery"), ignorance, hope, or spirit (*thumos*). As the *Eudemian Ethics* puts it, every virtue involves choice, which is of a goal, the beautiful (*EE* III 1230a27-29).

4.2 Temperance

Temperance is a virtue of character between intemperance and insensibility. The *Eudemian* discussion begins with two types of intemperance: the person who cannot be tempered, and the person who has not yet been tempered, a child. In the *Nicomachean Ethics,* Aristotle says that the appetitive part of the soul must chime with thought, both aiming at the beautiful (*EN* 1119b15-16). He compares the appetitive part with a child, but it is important to keep in mind that according to the *Eudemian* version, the child has not yet been tempered. In a virtuous adult, thought does not need to keep mistaken appetites in line.

Insensibility is a rare vice, according to Aristotle. Temperance, the virtue of character, relates to the pleasures of touch in sex and eating. One cannot be intemperate about smelling or seeing beautiful things. The *Nicomachean* discussion agrees on this point, but the restriction is puzzling. Although Aristotle would have been unaware of the phenomenon of binge watching, for example, he was aware of Plato's critique of those lovers of sights and sounds who are addicted to Dionysiac festivals (Plato's *Republic* V 475D-E).[57]

One interesting difference between the two discussions is the focus in the *Nicomachean Ethics* on whether cowardice and intemperance are voluntary (*EN* III 12 1119a21-33). He says that cowardice is more voluntary than cowardly acts, but intemperance is less voluntary than intemperate acts. The reason is that cowardly actions are caused by pain (fear), whereas cowardice is without pain, and that intemperate acts are caused by appetite, but no one has an appetite for being intemperate.

Perhaps Aristotle is more interested in this topic in the *Nicomachean Ethics*, because only there does he have a discussion about whether one's character is

---

[57] See Meinwald (2017) on "drama fiends" in Plato.

voluntary (*EN* III 5). However, it is not clear that the argument here is consistent with the earlier one. If one develops the disposition of cowardice by doing cowardly acts, why is cowardice not as voluntary or involuntary as those acts?

4.3 Generosity

The Greek term "*eleutheriotēs*" more literally means "liberality" than "generosity." The connection between generosity and freedom is that having property is the sign of a free person. Indeed, an enslaved person would be the property of another. Generosity comes between the vices of stinginess and wastefulness. The *Eudemian* discussion discusses the pleasure or pain the generous or bad people take in having or parting with their wealth, in line with its focus on the pleasure or pain people take in being virtuous or vicious. Different types of bad people are discussed, and Aristotle draws a distinction between the proper and two other uses of property: A shoe is used properly to walk, but coincidentally can be hired out for profit. The miser is only interested in the possession of money.

The *Nicomachean* version introduces the idea that the wasteful person may have several vices combined. Aristotle also expands on the idea that the generous person is someone who not merely gives to the right sources, but *takes* from the correct sources too. Pimps, usurers, and gamblers who take from their friends are not generous. It is a chastening idea that one cannot be generous with funds gained from exploiting others.

Aristotle also makes an interesting point about the possibility of changing one's character. As with temperance, Aristotle is more interested in whether one's character is voluntary in the *Nicomachean* than in the *Eudemian Ethics*. According to Aristotle, wasteful people, with guidance, can be led to the mean, whereas stingy people not so much, since old age exacerbates their bad character.

4.4 Magnificence

In the *Nicomachean Ethics*, magnificence follows generosity, whereas in the *Eudemian Ethics,* it follows magnanimity. Magnificience is a mean between niggardliness and ostentation. The *Eudemian Ethics* concentrates on entertaining others, for example, at a wedding, although he does also mention the way that politicians entertain their followers. The important point is that things must be suitable for the agent and for the occasion.

In the *Nicomachean Ethics*, tastefully privately funded public works are the paradigm cases of magnificence, although a child's toy can also count as magnificent, according to Aristotle. (In Athens, public works were required of very wealthy people.) (If one thinks that the *Nicomachean Ethics* is more directed toward legislators rather than philosophers, the difference in examples may be significant.)

4.5 Magnanimity and the Virtue Concerned with Honor on a Small Scale

According to Aristotle, in both works, the magnanimous person has all the virtues. Unlike the pusillanimous and the vain persons, the magnanimous person has the right view of his own abilities and character (self-knowledge), and puts himself forward for the great honors (not just respect from others, but also high offices in the city) he deserves. (This is a reasonable inference from the fact that those who have the vices shrink from the honors they deserve or put themselves forward for honors that they do not deserve.) In this way, the magnanimous person benefits the city more than the pusillanimous person, who deprives the city of her talents, and the vain person, who puts himself forward for honors he does not deserve. As Aristotle explains, honor is a particular concern of the magnanimous person (*EN* IV 3 1123b21-24).

While magnanimity is called "the crowning virtue," the magnanimous person is important in another way relating to Aristotle's triadic view of virtues and vices. While he has the correct view of himself, the pusillanimous person (with the deficiency vice) underestimates her own abilities and character while the vain person overestimates them. We earlier saw that Aristotle's triadic view of the virtues was puzzling, since there are often more vices than two that any given virtue comes between. Perhaps Aristotle wishes to emphasize three profiles in particular: people who think less of themselves than they should, people who will be prone to many vices of deficiency, and people who think more of themselves than they should, and so will be prone to vices of excess. In that case, there will be unity among the vices, just as there are among the virtues. Of course, there may still be characters who flip from one vice to another, like the rash coward, but, rather than detracting from the triadic view, they presuppose it.[58]

In the *Eudemian Ethics,* Aristotle describes a character who does not fit Aristotle's scheme, a person who is good enough to receive high honors but cannot put himself forward, perhaps because he is a resident alien. In the *Nicomachean Ethics*, there is a separate virtue for such a person, the virtue concerned with honor on a small scale, a virtue that comes between the vice of indifference to honor and the vice of being honor-loving. This virtue does not appear by itself in the *Eudemian Ethics*. Aristotle explains that there is a debate

---

[58] On the importance of self-knowledge in relation to magnanimity, the mean, and *akrasia*, see Gottlieb (2020), and on different kinds of bad people Gottlieb (2021, 109–113).

about whether it is better to be honor-loving or not, which is solved when one sees that there is a virtue in the mean.

4.6 Calmness

Calmness ("*praotēs*") refers to another nameless virtue of character in Aristotle's *Nicomachean Ethics*. Since it is at the top of Aristotle's list of nameless virtues, I shall examine it in more detail than the others. It is a mean related to the feeling of anger (*orgē*) (*EN* IV 5 1125b30). Aristotle says that its opposing vices of excess and deficiency are practically nameless as well, although he calls the vices "a sort of irascibility (*orgilotēs tis*)" and "a sort of inirascibility (*aorgēsia tis*)."[59]

Aristotle says that "we refer 'calmness' to the mean, inclining to the deficiency, being nameless" (*EN* IV 5 1125b27). The Greek term translated "calmness" does not quite fit the virtue of character to be explained, because the name, like my translation, implies a lack of anger. There is no clear English term for the person who is angry when he should, toward whom he should, and so forth, where these vary from circumstance to circumstance so that it may be appropriate to be very angry on one occasion and not at all on another, just as there is none in the Greek.

These terminological issues aside, one might wonder whether there are other reasons why this virtue of character counts as nameless, apart from the fact that the name Aristotle gives it does not quite fit. After all, some of Aristotle's named virtues could be criticized for the same reason. One approach would be to look at other authors before and contemporary with Aristotle and see what they are referring to when they use the term.[60] Another, which I shall take in what follows, is to look to Aristotle himself.

A possible explanation why the four other nameless virtues in the *Nicomachean Ethics* – the virtue concerning honor on a small scale, truthfulness, wittiness, and friendliness – are nameless is given by the fact that they do not count as virtues of character in the *Eudemian Ethics*. The virtue concerning honor on a small scale is not discussed at all, whereas the other virtues are not virtues of character because they are all temperamental means and are without choice (*prohairesis*) (*EE* 6 1234a24-26) as I mentioned in Section 2. Whatever the case, this explanation does not apply to calmness because it *is* included in the

---

[59] Christopher Taylor notes that although the terms "*praotēs*," "*praos*," and "*orgilos*" were in current use, "*orgilotēs*," "*aorgēsia*," and "*aorgētos*" do not occur in extant texts before their use here, and he conjectures that at least the last two are Aristotelian coinages (Taylor 2006, 118).

[60] Nikolaidis (1982, 420) concludes that Aristotle's predecessors thought that calmness was utter meekness.

Eudemian account. It is the only nameless virtue that counts as a virtue of character in that work, although it is not called nameless in that work.[61]

However, in Aristotle's *Rhetoric* (*Rh.*), calmnness, along with the other nameless virtues, is missing from Aristotle's list of virtues (*Rh.* I 9 1366b1-3). In the *Rhetoric,* it is classified, with friendliness, as a feeling (*pathos*) in Aristotle's list of feelings. In the *De Anima* too, it seems to be mentioned briefly as a *pathos* (*De Anima* I 403a16-18).

In the *Rhetoric*, Aristotle lists the feelings as pairs of opposites, for example, fear is opposed to confidence, shame to shamelessness, pity to indignation, and so on. Aristotle defines anger as an impulse involving pain for revenge because of an apparent slight toward oneself or what concerns one's friends, when the slight is not fitting (*Rh.* II 2 1378a30-32).[62] According to Aristotle, getting angry is opposed to calming down, and anger is opposed to calmness (*Rh.* II 3 1380a6-9).

According to Aristotle, there are cases that do and ought to make someone calm down, for example, finding out that the perpetrator of a slight did it involuntarily. Others are cases that do make people calm down, but are not necessarily rational, for example, having one's anger for one person extinguished by venting anger on someone else the day before. Aristotle describes a case where the Athenians are very angry with Ergophilos, but since they condemned Callisthenes to death the day before, they spared Ergophilos on the next day (*Rh.* II 3 1380b10-14).

Again, some are cases in which people calm down after being angry, for example, finding out that the perpetrator feels regret, while some are cases where the perpetrator has already suffered enough so that there is no need to take revenge. Other cases are those where one should not get angry in the first place, for example, cases in which the person one is engaging with is not the sort of person who would show disrespect. Such a person behaves humbly toward one, or takes one seriously or is someone one respects. Aristotle also presents cases where one is calm even though one need not have been angry before, for example, while attending a play or a feast.

At the end of the chapter, Aristotle provides a selective summary of his account, "Clearly, then, those wishing to calm down [an audience] should speak from these topics; they produce such a feeling in them by having made

---

[61] It is also a virtue in the *Magna Moralia* (*MM* I xxii 1191b24-39). The author of that work says that he will leave the question whether the means he mentions (including the nameless ones of the *Nicomachean Ethics*) are virtues or not for another discussion (*MM.* I xxxii 1193a37-40). This promise is never fulfilled in that work.

[62] Translations of the *Rhetoric* are based on Kennedy (1991) with major revisions. For more on anger, see Scheiter (2012a).

them regard those with whom they are angry as either persons to be feared or worthy of respect or benefactors or involuntary actors or as very grieved by what they have done" (*Rh.* II 3 1380b31-34).

Let us suppose that calmness is the result of calming down after getting angry, or a frame of mind in which one is unlikely to get angry. Neither of these correctly describes the virtue called "calmness" in the *Nicomachean* and *Eudemian Ethics*. First of all, the person with the virtue of character, calmness, does not need to have been angry previously to exercise the virtue. Second, the person with the virtue of character, calmness, is not necessarily calm all the time. According to Aristotle's doctrine of the mean, the calm person is angry at the appropriate people on the appropriate occasions and so forth. If Aristotle thinks that calmness is an apt name for the phenomena in the *Rhetoric*, he would therefore be justified in saying that what counts as calmness in the *Nicomachean* and *Eudemian Ethics* in fact has no name, although he is giving it the name of "calmness" as a courtesy. (I shall suggest a further explanation for the name-lessness of the nameless virtues in the conclusion to this book.)

Despite the differences between the accounts in the *Rhetoric* and in the ethical works, there is one interesting point of contact with the *Nicomachean* account. In the *Rhetoric,* Aristotle says that people will calm down toward those with whom they are angry if they think that the slight that triggered the anger was involuntary. In the *Nicomachean Ethics*, we shall see that the person with the virtue of calmness is someone who is prone to sympathetic consideration (*suggnōmē*), making allowances for that and other mitigating circumstances.

There are two important differences between the accounts of calmness in the *Eudemian* and *Nicomachean Ethics* (*EN* IV 5 and *EE* III 3). First, the *Nicomachean Ethics* specifically mentions thought, and second, it includes a comment about sympathetic consideration and revenge that is missing from the parallel discussion in the *Eudemian Ethics*.

Aristotle writes: "For being a calm person means not being disturbed i.e. (*kai*), not being led by feeling, but getting angry in the way, about the things and for the length of time that thought prescribes" (*EN* IV 5 1125b33-1126a1).[63]

I have treated the word "*kai*" as "i.e.," rather than "and," which is possible in Greek, because the calm person is not undisturbed period, but is someone who is not led merely by feeling. Thought prescribes the way, time, and so forth that one should be angry. Here what is important is the emphasis on thought as well as feeling. My hypothesis is that at this point in the *Nicomachean Ethics*, where the nameless virtues are all full virtues of character involving choice and

---

[63] For an argument to the effect that anger as a desire for retaliation is *never* warranted, see Nussbaum (2015).

presumably also thoughtfulness, Aristotle wants to emphasize the thoughtful side to the virtue of calmness. Hence the inclusion of this paragraph here.

The very same passage continues as follows: "He (the calm person) seems to err more to the deficiency, for the calm person is not prone to revenge, but rather is prone to sympathetic consideration (*suggnōmonikos*)" (*EN* IV 5 1126a1-3). There is no mention of sympathetic consideration in the parallel passage in the *Eudemian Ethics*, although Aristotle does note that it is possible to go to excess in the direction of the gentle (*ileōn*) and placable (*katallaktikon*) in an earlier discussion of the virtues (*EE* II 6 1222b1-2). As we saw, sympathetic consideration played a more prominent role in the discussion of the voluntary in the *Nicomachean Ethics*. It appears again, in conjunction with thoughtfulness and fair-mindedness, in the common book *EN* V/*EE* VI.

In his *Nicomachean* chapter on calmness, Aristotle explains that how far one should deviate from the mean (here what one should do and feel in a particular case) cannot be defined by thought (*logos*), but is a matter of discernment (*krisis*), which depends on perception of particulars (*EN* II IV 5 1126b cf. II 9 1109b20-23). Perception of particulars also plays an important role in *EE* V/*EN* VI and *EE* VI/*EN* VII.

If calmness is connected with sympathetic consideration and sympathetic consideration with fair-mindedness, it turns out that the ancient historian Thucydides agrees. He complains that in the Peloponnesian war the Athenians lacked the fair-mindedness to retain the allegiance of their allies, whereas the Spartan general Brasidas who had calmness was able to keep the Spartan allies on his side. Brasidas is the only person whom Thucydides praises for this quality, another reason perhaps why it is nameless among the Athenians.[64]

4.7 Friendliness

While friendliness is a nameless virtue in the *Nicomachean Ethics*, it does not count as a virtue in the *Eudemian Ethics*. In the *Eudemian Ethics,* friendliness is a temperamental mean between animosity (*echthra*) and flattery (*kolakeia*). According to the *Eudemian Ethics*, the one who falls in readily with every desire is a flatterer, the one who objects to every desire is quarrelsome, and the one who does not fall in with nor oppose every desire but goes along with what appears to be best is friendly.

In the chart of virtues of character in the *Nicomachean Ethics*, Aristotle says that the person who is pleasant to others as he should be is friendly. A person who goes to excess is ingratiating (*areskos*) if he has no ulterior motive, and

---

[64] See Romilly (1974).

a flatterer (*kolax*) if he acts for his own benefit. The deficient person, unpleasant in everything, will be a sort of quarrelsome and ill-tempered person (*EN* II 7 1108a27-31).

The later chapter repeats the distinction between the ingratiating person and the flatterer. The friendly person accepts or objects to things as he should (*EN* IV 6 1126b19-20), sharing pleasure or giving pain when necessary, in relation to the beautiful. He will behave differently toward those with a (correct) reputation for worth, and differently toward those he knows and toward strangers (*EN* IV 6 1126b35-36). For example, it would be inappropriate to greet a complete stranger with a big hug.

While friendliness is a temperamental mean without choice in the *Eudemian Ethics*, in the *Nicomachean Ethics*, Aristotle comments by contrast:

> For friendliness seems to be about pleasures and pains that arise in gatherings. In such cases, where it is not beautiful or harmful to share pleasure, the friendly person will object, and choose (*proairēsetai*) to cause pain.
>
> (*EN* IV 6 1126b30-33)[65]

4.8 Dignity

In the *Eudemian Ethics*, there is a separate temperamental mean of dignity (*semnotēs*), or perhaps being dignified, since dignity in modern parlance is less about how one relates to others. The discussion overlaps with the discussion of friendliness, since Aristotle uses the same term "ingratiating" that he used for a vice connected with friendliness, for the deficient propensity. While Aristotle does discuss the good person's relation to those who are worthy in his discussion of friendliness in the *Nicomachean Ethics*, the focus is pleasure or pain, and the beautiful, not specifically mentioned in the account of dignity:

> Dignity is a mean between arrogance (*authadeia*) and being ingratiating (*areskeia*). Someone who leads a life looking down on others is arrogant, whereas the one who looks to another in everything and is subservient to all is ingratiating. The one who is dignified defers in some matters but not others, and in relation to those who are worthy. (*EE* III 7 1233b29-38)

This mean is interesting for both its connections with the magnanimous person's attitude to others, and with the virtue of thought, comprehension, which relates to assessing others' speech on issues that concern thoughtfulness (*EE* V/*EN* VI 10). Perhaps it is missing in the *Nicomachean Ethics* because it is no longer needed as a separate propensity.

---

[65] See Meyer (2016) for the role of *to kalon* (the beautiful) in Aristotle's treatment of friendliness in the *EN*.

4.9 Truthfulness

According to the *Nicomachean Ethics*, truthfulness is a nameless virtue concerned with telling the truth about oneself, coming between boastfulness (literally, crowing, like a rooster) and self-deprecation. It differs from sincerity, since that does not entail that one's opinions about oneself are correct. While truthfulness is not a Homeric virtue, since the Homeric heroes and gods often disguise who they are and do not tell the truth about themselves, it is an Aristotelian virtue. Tact may dictate what truths it is appropriate for the truthful person to relate to whom and on what occasions, so telling the whole truth and nothing but the truth is not an Aristotelian imperative.[66]

While in the *Eudemian Ethics* Aristotle says that there are no opposing vices to these means (*EE* III 7 1234a24-25), in the *Nicomachean Ethics* he takes pains to show that boastfulness involves choice:

> Someone is not a boaster with regard to capacity (*en tēi dunamei*), but with regard to choice (*en tēi proairesei*). For in accord with one's disposition and by being that sort of person, someone is a boaster (*EN* IV 7 1127b14-15).

In the *Nicomachean Ethics*, truthful people are truthful in word and life, not exaggerating or diminishing their own qualities (*EN* IV 7), whereas in the *Eudemian Ethics,* they are described as being blunt, calling each thing what it is (*authekaston*), which sounds more like a matter of temperament (*EE* III 7 1233b38).

It is noteworthy Aristotle claims that it is worse to boast for gain, for example, claiming to be a physician when one is not, than just sounding off. Here again, the scope of a nameless virtue and the corresponding vices go beyond the private sphere.

4.10 Wit

The witty person comes between the boor and the buffoon. Wit is an ethical disposition since the witty person makes and listens to jokes as he should. Aristotle describes wit as mental agility (*epidexiotēs*) comparable to physical agility. That is one reason that innuendo is preferable to out and out abuse (*EN* IV 8 1128a16-25). Hurling insults in comedy is not as good (or as educational) as satire, and presumably satire should be directed at the appropriate people too. By contrast, in the *Eudemian Ethics*, for example, wit and its associated bad

---

[66] Given this account of truthfulness in the *Nicomachean Ethics*, and the way its expression varies in different circumstances, it would not seem to be a purely intellectual virtue, although, of course, it requires the virtue of thought, which is thoughtfulness (*phronēsis*). Thanks to Giulia Bonasio for raising this point.

conditions are compared with types of eating, where the boor is like a picky eater, and the buffoon (on the side of excess) is like a person who eats everything indiscriminately (*EE* III 7 1234a4-8). The analogy suggests that moderation would be the correct condition, a misleading way of understanding the doctrine of the mean.

Interestingly, in the *Nicomachean Ethics*, Aristotle suggests that since legislators prohibit some types of abuse, they should prohibit some types of jokes also (*EN* IV 8 1128a30-31). This claim belies the idea that the nameless virtues concern private as opposed to public morality.

4.11 Shame and Proper Indignation (*Nemesis*)

In the *Nicomachean Ethics*, Aristotle lists only two temperamental means, shame and proper indignation, although, as we shall see, these are described differently in the *Eudemian Ethics*.

Shame, he says, is not a virtue, although it is a praiseworthy mean between being bashful and shameless. In the *Eudemian Ethics,* it is also a temperamental mean between two other propensities. Aristotle says that the one who does not care what anyone thinks is shameless, the one who pays attention to everyone's view similarly is bashful, and the one who cares for the opinion of those who appear decent is prone to shame (*EE* II 7 1233b26-29). He also says that shame contributes to temperance (*sōphrosunē*) (*EN* III 7 1234a32), a puzzling comment if temperance is the same virtue discussed earlier on, as opposed to sobriety in general. Indeed, it seems more appropriate to the kind of modesty and self-knowledge discussed in Plato's *Charmides*. Charmides, who has a bashful temperament, is there a suitable interlocutor for a dialogue on *sōphrosunē*.

The *Nicomachean* account has a different focus (*EN* IV 9). First, Aristotle says that shame is more like a feeling, as it makes people blush. Then he explains that while young people are praised for being prone to shame when they go astray, older people should not feel shame because they should not do things that they would be ashamed of. Aristotle agrees with the counterfactual claim that if a person did shameful things they would feel ashamed, but says that that does not apply to the virtues. The good person would not do anything to be ashamed of. Aristotle says nothing about prospective shame being a main motivator for the virtuous person. As we saw in the discussion of bravery, being disposed to act merely to avoid shame does not count as true virtue. Young people, according to Aristotle, are praised for retrospective shame. He does not mention praise for their acting correctly due to the possibility of prospective shame. When Aristotle later says that the many naturally obey fear, not shame, he is not praising shame as a virtue, but pointing out that the many care only about penalties, and not about the ugly things that they should be ashamed of (*EN* X 9 1179b11-13). *Nicomachean* shame seems to be more about what one should be ashamed of than the people in front of whom one should feel shame.[67]

The *Nicomachean Ethics* has a short comment on proper indignation (*nemesis*) that is between envy (*phthonos*) and schadenfreude (*epichairekakia*).[68] The properly indignant person feels pain at those who do well undeservedly, the envious person exceeds him at feeling pained at everyone's good fortune, while the person prone to schadenfreude is so deficient in feeling pain that he rejoices at others' misfortune (*EN* II 7 1108a35-36). Aristotle never fulfills his promise to discuss this propensity later on in the *Nicomachean Ethics*, unless the discussion has been lost.

This is one of the few cases where a propensity is discussed at greater length in the *Eudemian Ethics*. As in the *Nicomachean Ethics,* the person prone to proper indignation comes between the envious person and the person prone to schadenfreude. The envious person is pained when people do well deservedly, while the person prone to schadenfreude feels pleasure at undeserved misfortunes.

However, Aristotle makes the puzzling claim that the feeling of the person prone to schadenfreude is nameless, and that the envious and those prone to schadenfreude are so called in relation to their dispositions (*hexeis*). I take it that the latter claim is Aristotle's way of stressing that he is not just discussing those who are envious or have schadenfreude on a single occasion, not that he means to say that these are the sort of dispositions that have the reliability of virtues and vices.

Interestingly, Plato calls the feeling of enjoyment at the misfortunes of others, especially characters in a comedy, "*phthonos*" (*Philebus* 49 C-50E), the term Aristotle uses for envy. As we saw earlier, Aristotelian envy (*phthonos*) is not schadenfreude. Perhaps Aristotle thinks that schadenfreude is nameless because he is drawing a distinction between the two that was not clear in ordinary Greek.[69]

In the *Rhetoric*, his most detailed account of the feelings, Aristotle says of sympathy:

---

[67] For a more charitable view of the role of shame, see Marta Jimenez (2021).

[68] Taylor suggests "schadenfreude" but prefers "spite" as being more suitable for an English translation (Taylor 2006, 120). However, spite involves acting on one's feelings in a way that schadenfreude does not, and spiteful people do not necessarily aim their spite only at people who are doing badly.

[69] Thanks to Emily Fletcher for discussion of these points. On the difficulty of treating *nemesis* as a mean at all, see Mills (1985) and Leighton (2011).

> *Let sympathy (eleos) be a certain pain at something that strikes one as*
> *harmful, destructive or painful, that befalls one who does not deserve it*
> *(tou anaxiou)* and which we might expect to befall ourselves or some friend
> of ours, and moreover to befall us soon. (*Rh.* II 8 1385b13-16) (my emphasis)

The *Eudemian* version of proper indignation is broader than the *Nicomachean*, since it includes an element of sympathy, pain at someone who does badly undeservedly. Proper indignation also includes pleasure at those who do well. Proper *indignation*, then, is not the whole story in the *Eudemian Ethics*. Aristotle says:

> The person prone to proper indignation (the *nemēsetikos*) which the ancients called "nemesis," is pained at bad doings and good doings that are undeserved, and rejoices at deserved things. For this reason, people think Nemesis is a god. (*EE* III 7 1233b23-26)

Perhaps people think that *nemesis* is a god because only a god would be able to put such fortunes and misfortunes to rights as a kind of avenging angel. Indeed, in the *Eudemian Ethics*, Aristotle says that *nemesis* contributes to the virtue of justice (*EE* III 7 1234a31-32). *Nemesis* is not explicitly mentioned in Aristotle's book on justice, which is a common book. As we shall see, according to Aristotle, there is general justice, which is the whole of ethical virtue in relation to another, and two types of particular justice: rectificatory and political.[70] Given the focus of special justice on victims being compensated for wrongdoing, and everyone having their fair share, it is reasonable to suppose that the person who has righteous indignation will be indignant when a wrong is not righted or when some have more than their fair share, situations that they do not deserve, and pleased when things go as they should, and that these attitudes will contribute to being just.

4.12 Endurance

Endurance does not appear in the *Nicomachean* list of virtues, but it does appear in the *Eudemian* list of means, although not in the expanded discussion. It makes a cameo appearance in the common book (*EE* VI/*EN* VII) in the discussion of *akrasia*. There Aristotle says that he will consider *akrasia* and *enkrateia* along with softness and endurance (*EE* VI/*EN* VII 1 1145a35-36) and he compares the akratic with the soft person, and the enkratic with the enduring

---

[70] Aristotle says that general and particular justice are homonymous, by which he means that what it is to be general justice is as different from what it is to be special justice as what it is to be a bank (of a river) is different from what it is to be a bank (where one deposits money). On homonymy, see Aristotle's *Categories* 1 1a1-6.

one (*EE* VI/*EN* VII 7 1150a32-1150b5). These comparisons cast doubt on the idea that endurance is ever a virtue, according to Aristotle.[71]

5 Justice

Justice is the topic of the first of the so-called common books. All but one of the extant manuscripts of Aristotle's *Eudemian Ethics* share three books in common with the *Nicomachean Ethics*.[72] As we have them, *Eudemian Ethics* IV–VI are the same as *Nicomachean Ethics* V–VII. These so-called common books, though, are far from common in the works of any author. It is indeed a puzzle how two works could have three books in common. Did Aristotle or an editor decide to put them in both works, and, if they originally belonged to the *Eudemian Ethics*, as many assume, were they revised mostly or in part to fit in the *Nicomachean Ethics*?[73] These issues are hotly debated by scholars.[74] While my aim is not to resolve these issues, I shall note the presence of *Eudemian* and *Nicomachean* ideas, namely, ideas that are more prominent in either of the indisputably *Eudemian* and *Nicomachean* books, as I proceed. For the sake of clarity, I shall therefore continue to use the terms "*Eudemian*" and "*Nicomachean*" for the noncommon books.

Aristotle's discussion of justice covers a variety of topics, including different types of justice, justice in economic exchange (exchange value), voluntary action, whether one can do injustice to oneself, and fair-mindedness (*epieikeia*) (often also translated as "decency" or "equity").[75] He starts by distinguishing general justice, which is the whole of virtue as it relates to another, and two types of particular justice – rectificatory justice, the sort of justice that rectifies particular unjust acts in the setting of a law court, and distributive justice, which

---

[71] Cf. Gottlieb (2009, 78–79).

[72] For further details, see the preface to Rowe (forthcoming).

[73] Also, if so, how did only the revised versions become parts of the *Eudemian* manuscript tradition?

[74] In the twentieth century, Jaeger (1923) set the stage with his developmental view of Aristotle's works. Kenny (1978) argued on stylometric and other grounds that the common books are all of *Eudemian* origin (and later than the *Nicomachean Ethics*). Primavesi (2007) argues that they are *Nicomachean*, based on the numbers of the books of each work in the ancient catalogues. Rowe (1971) and Devereux (2014) argue, although for different reasons, that *EE* V/*EN* VI is closer to the *Nicomachean* than to *the Eudemian Ethics*. Rowe (2022) now thinks that it is *sophia* rather than *phronēsis* in the *EE* which differs from the *EN*, including *EE* V/*EN* VI: *Sophia* in the *EE* has broader scope. Lorenz (2009a) argues that the *Eudemian* books have been revised for a later *Nicomachean* home. For example, he argues that *EE* VI/*EN* VII 6 contains both a *Eudemian* and a *Nicomachean* version of the argument (Lorenz 2009b). Kenny (2016, 304) argues against his claims. Pakaluk (2011) addresses problems about the unity of the *Nicomachean Ethics*, arguing that Aristotle or one or more editors of the *Nicomachean Ethics* do not mention book I or key parts of the common books. Frede (2019) argues for a *Nicomachean* origin of the common books, especially the book on justice.

[75] Striker (2006) considers justice as basic. See Mi-Kyong (Mitzi) Lee for a detailed discussion of justice as the basis of Aristotle's ethics (Lee in press).

is of political import – and varies according to the organization of the polis. (The discussion of this type of justice relies on mathematical proportions, perhaps more fitting for a Eudemian treatment.) While this may sound like a relativist position, Aristotle makes sure to distinguish natural and conventional justice. Natural justice, like a burning fire, is the same everywhere.

The motive for injustice, according to Aristotle, is aiming at more than one's fair share or greed (*pleonexia*). Aristotle's account of justice is arguably directed at Thrasymachus, Socrates's nemesis in Plato's *Republic*, who argued in favor of unbridled greed and claimed that justice is another's good. However, whereas Thrasymachus claimed that it was no good at all to the doer, on Aristotle's view, since general justice includes all the virtues of character necessary for a happy life, the agent will be benefitted too.

A crux of the book is that particular justice is not in a mean like the other virtues of character, since it concerns an intermediate position between two states of affairs, having too much for oneself while others have too little, and having too little oneself while others have too much.[76] According to Aristotle, one cannot do injustice to oneself (perhaps a remnant of the Socratic view that no one errs willingly), so the deficiency vice is not possible. It is noteworthy that Aristotle nevertheless concludes that justice is also a virtue of character, and he does not show any inkling that this type of mean vitiates his view of the mean in general. Perhaps that is because there is a disposition of fair-mindedness (*epieikeia*) which, although the same as justice, is better than one way of being just. It is a disposition to stick to the spirit and not just the letter of the law, when the law, by its universal nature, may on occasion miss the mark. This seems to capture exactly the mentality of the person whose character is in a mean. Such a person takes account of the particular circumstances, and is not hidebound by inflexible rules. In the following book we will see the relationship between fair-mindedness and sympathetic consideration, a prominent attitude in the *Nicomachean* discussion of the voluntary, and other virtues of thought related to thoughtfulness (*phronēsis*).

Following John Rawls, modern philosophers are apt to consider justice a virtue of institutions as opposed to people, but Aristotle would note that it is people with certain priorities that create and perpetuate those institutions. If those institutions are unjust, it is fair-minded people who are needed to change them.

We might be surprised to see yet another account of the voluntary in the middle of a discussion of justice, but the taxonomy of different types of offences is naturally at home here. The description of the particulars of voluntary action

---

[76] On Aristotle on inequality of wealth, see Gottlieb (2018).

fits both the *Nicomachean* view and the concluding definition of the voluntary in the *Eudemian* version, but Aristotle's talk of natural processes (aging is not voluntary or involuntary, for example) is reminiscent of the *Eudemian* account. Aristotle expands on the *Eudemian* distinction between doing something unjust by accident versus doing it voluntarily and puts forward a further distinction between performing an unjust act and being an unjust person.[77] Someone who does an unjust act out of anger is not an unjust person. While he acts voluntarily, he does not act by choice, and so his action is of a different caliber. These distinctions might be helpful in sorting out the puzzle of *Nicomachean Ethics* II 4, where it appeared that one could not do a just act of any kind without being a just person.

Aristotle makes a few extra points that are worthy of note. In order to do injustice to another person, one's action must be against that person's wish. Since, according to Aristotle, no one voluntarily suffers injustice, suicide counts as an injustice against one's society. Aristotle half agrees with Socrates, saying that doing injustice is worse than suffering it, although the latter may be a larger misfortune.

Contra Hobbes and others, according to Aristotle, justice is not an artificial virtue, going against the grain of humans' natural desires and developed according to a social contract.[78] According to Aristotle, human beings are naturally more cooperative than the social animals like bees, not less so, as Hobbes claims.

6 Virtues of Thought

The second common book, *Eudemian Ethics* V/*Nicomachean Ethics* VI begins with a problem about the elucidation of virtue and the mean.[79] In his *Eudemian Ethics*, after discussing the virtues of character, and saying that they are in accord with the correct thought (*kata ton orthon logon*), Aristotle promises "Later we must inquire what the correct thought is and what is the standard (*horos*) we should look to in saying <what> the mean is" (*EE* II 5 1222b7-9).[80] Aristotle therefore seems to be following up on this *Eudemian* point when he asks in this common book what "is the target (*skopos*) looking to which the person having thought stretches and relaxes, and what is the standard (*horos*) of

---

[77] For a full discussion of accidental action and production, see Meyer (2012, 100–121).

[78] On the view that the virtues are not essentially remedial (intended to remedy intrinsically bad feelings), see Gottlieb (2009, 53–57; 2021, 34–36).

[79] See Peterson (1992) on the problem of circularity.

[80] The term "*horos*" is only found in the *Eudemian* and common books. It can also mean "definition" (Irwin 2019), "limit" (Woods 1992), or "mark" (Simpson 2013).

the means, which we say are the means between excess and deficiency, being in accord with the correct thought" (*EE* V/*EN* VI 1 1138b20-25).

The Greek is difficult, but the point about stretching and relaxing is a musical metaphor too and so also resonates with the *Nicomachean* point that the person who is in the mean is "tuned" correctly, neither too slackly nor too intensely, so as to feel and act correctly (*EN* II 1105b25-28), that is, to hit the mean.[81] (This point relates to the idea that the good person's character is balanced, or in equilibrium.)

The main problem, as Aristotle explains it, is that saying that virtue is in a mean as defined by the person with thoughtfulness (*phronēsis*) is no more helpful than saying that medical treatment is "what medicine (*hē iatrikē*) prescribes and in the manner of (*hōs*) the person who has this" (*EE* V/*EN* VI 1 1138b31-32). Saying that is "true, but not at all clear" or enlightening.[82] This problem applies to Aristotle's comment in the *Nicomachean Ethics* that "[v]irtue of character is a prohairetic disposition, being in a mean relative to us, defined by the thought (*logos*), i.e., by the thought by which the person with thoughtfulness (*ho phronimos*) would define it" (*EN* II 6 1106b36-1107a2). (An alternative manuscript says "in the manner of (*hōs*) the person with thoughtfulness," the same as the turn of phrase used in the common book.) The problem also applies to Aristotle's comments in the *Eudemian Ethics* that the mean is "the way in which (*hōs*) knowledge (*epistēmē*) and thought (*ho logos*) orders" (*EE* II 1220b28), and, in the context of magnanimity, that "Each particular virtue discriminates correctly between the greater and the lesser, as the person with thoughtfulness, and virtue, prescribe" (*EN* III 5 1232a35-38).

Next Aristotle divides the part of the soul that has thought (*logos*) (minus the part that is responsive to thought) into two parts: one dealing with practical thought and one dealing with theoretical thought. The former has as its objects contingent matters, whereas the latter is concerned with necessary truths. This distinction is not found explicitly in the earlier books of either the *Nicomachean* or *Eudemian Ethics*, although, as previously shown, it is foreshadowed in the account of choice. The role of this paragraph is disputed. It could be a new introduction or merely further elaboration of the purview of thoughtfulness.

On the topic of truth, we have a new discussion of what Aristotle calls "practical truth" (*EE* V/*EN* VI 2 1139a26).[83] Here Aristotle makes the striking comment that choice (of the good person) is desiderative thought or thoughtful desire (*EE* V/*EN* VI 2 1139b4-5). On my view, this is his way of saying that choice, the phenomenon of *prohairesis*, of the good person is deliberation, wish,

---

[81] For more on this important point, see Gottlieb (2021, 136–137).

[82] "Clear" is Aristotle's term, an ancestor of Descartes's "clear and distinct ideas."

[83] On this topic, see Anscombe (1965) and, most recently, Olfert (2017).

and desires from the feelings, all merged together, with none lording it over the others.[84] As Aristotle says in the *Eudemian* discussion of the voluntary, it is the whole soul that is the origin of action (*EE* II 8 1224b27-28).

Next, Aristotle distinguishes various virtues of thought. The virtue of wisdom (*sophia*) is a combination of scientific knowledge (*epistēmē*) and understanding (*nous*). According to Aristotle, those who have scientific knowledge can demonstrate that knowledge from first principles. Demonstration entails giving a sound deductive argument from first principles, where the conclusion is explained by the premises. Understanding is what grasps first principles, although it may itself be a result of induction. Aristotle refers to his *Analytics*, an early work, for more details (e.g., *Posterior Analytics* I 2), going a step further from his discussion on choice.

Aristotle goes on to distinguish thoughtfulness from these virtues of thought and also from skill (*technē*), a distinction that is blurred both at the beginning and at the end of the *Nicomachean Ethics* where "*epistēmē*" also includes skill (*EN* I 1 1094b2-5, *EN* II 6 1106b8-12, and *EN* X 1180b15-16). One might conclude from this that those parts of the *Nicomachean Ethics* were written independently of this common book.

Aristotle distinguishes action, the purview of thoughtfulness, and production, the purview of skill. Action is done for its own sake, whereas production has an object beyond itself, a product. The distinction may appear puzzling, especially given Aristotle's constant use of analogies between the good person and skilled professionals, for example, the harpist or the physician.[85] Much ink has been spilled trying to understand Aristotle's metaphysical distinction between process and activity. Perhaps a more fruitful and charitable way of understanding Aristotle's claim is as saying that the person with thoughtfulness lacks a "product mentality." Despite what he says, physicians need not have product mentalities either. A physician without a product mentality would not view those she treats as "customers," just as a university administrator without a product mentality would not view the point of education as a list of "outcomes" for student "consumers." According to Aristotle (as explained in *EN* II 4), virtuous actions are not evaluated by mere outcomes: A soldier may be brave even though his side fails to win a victory. Aristotle excludes artisans from being citizens because he assumes that artisans must have product mentalities. I leave it to the reader to consider whether that is true.

Another way in which thoughtfulness differs from skill is that it cannot be forgotten or misused. Aristotle defines thoughtfulness as a "true practical

---

[84] For a full defense of this claim, see Gottlieb (2021).
[85] For a longer discussion, see Gottlieb (2009, 153–156).

disposition involving thought concerning human goods" (*EN VI/EE* V 5 1140b20-21).

Aristotle distinguishes different types of thoughtfulness, applying to functions of the polis, household management, legislation, and political thoughtfulness, which can be deliberative or judicial. This provides a segue into his discussion of good deliberation and virtues of thought required for the polis: comprehension (*sunesis*) needed to follow speeches in the assembly and law courts, and consideration (*gnōmē*), a trait related to sympathetic consideration and fair-mindedness, that appeared in the Athenian jurors' oath. Jurors were required to swear to judge in accordance with the laws and that on matters where the law is silent, "to decide by their own most just consideration" (Demosthenes, *Against Leptines* 118).[86]

A distinctive feature of all these traits is that they focus on particulars, for example, "this is the time to act," "this is a person in need," as well as universals (but where universals are "for the most part" only), for example, "generous people generally help friends in need." (The examples are my own.) Aristotle's practical syllogism, described as "one of Aristotle's best discoveries" by Elizabeth Anscombe (1957), makes this point clear. While "Generous people generally help friends in need" is the major premise, action requires indexical thoughts, and, in order to lead to action, the agent must also have the appropriate virtue of character. The minor premise says "this is my friend in need" and also includes "I am a generous person," a fact that explains her action, but is not something that she thinks to herself.[87]

A different type of understanding (*nous*) which is practical informs the discussion.[88] It was not introduced in the earlier taxonomy of virtues of thought.

The final part of the book raises various puzzles about the point of thoughtfulness and wisdom and the relationship between thoughtfulness and virtue of character. Aristotle makes the much debated claim that virtue makes the goal correct, while thoughtfulness makes the things that contribute to the goal correct (a claim he also accepts at *EE* II 11 1227b23-24, and which I discussed in Section 3).[89] However, that would seem to contradict his claim in the same book that thoughtfulness is the true grasp of the goal (*EN* VI 9 1142b31-33). The solution is that both together make the goal correct, as both are needed for all stages of ethical practical thinking.[90]

Aristotle argues that virtue of character and thoughtfulness require each other. Although we can have one natural virtue without another, we cannot

---

[86] See Stewart (1892) and Gifford (1995).

[87] For a detailed account of this view, see Gottlieb (2006; 2009, 151–172).

[88] See Whiting (1986).

[89] See Moss (2011), Price (2011), and Coope (2012).

[90] See too Gottlieb (2021, 64).

have one virtue proper without all the rest.[91] Aristotle refers forward to this passage in his discussion of virtue of character in the *Eudemian Ethics* when explaining how the temperamental means may contribute to natural virtues, but the point being made here seems to be different. The notion that if we strip away thoughtfulness from proper virtue we are left with natural virtue, just as if we strip away virtue of character from thoughtfulness, we are left with the capacity of cleverness, is a thought experiment.[92] Even if we are naturally just, brave, prone to temperance, and so forth immediately from birth, whether these natural virtues can really be virtues – how can they hit the mean without thoughtfulness? – is dubious, to say the least.

In any event, here Aristotle seems to provide one way of addressing the original question of this book concerning the standard (*horos*) or target (*skopos*) of the thoughtful person. The question is misguided.[93] The correct thought (*orthos logos*) just is thoughtfulness. Furthermore, virtue of character is not merely in accord with the correct thought, but involves the correct thought (*meta tou orthou logou*). In order to have virtue of character, one must have a "metalog mentality" where, contra Socrates, the thought and feeling of the good person are interdependent. Someone can be healthy just by consulting a physician. A good person, by contrast, must have his own thoughts integrated with his feelings in order to be good.[94] Even if, per impossibile, one could provide an algorithm for the good person to follow, merely doing what it said would not by itself make one a good person.

Regarding the relationship between thoughtfulness and wisdom, according to Aristotle, both thoughtfulness and wisdom are choiceworthy in themselves because they are both virtues and therefore contribute to happiness (their exercise). At the very end of the book, Aristotle comments that

> thoughtfulness does not control wisdom or the better part of the soul, just as medicine does not use health, but brings health into being. Therefore it prescribes for the sake of health, but does not prescribe to health. This <i.e., saying otherwise> would be like saying that politics rules the gods because it prescribes about everything in the city. (*EE* V/*EN* VI 1145b6-11)

The point of these dark sayings seems to be that while thoughtfulness prescribes, among other things, when or where one should activate one's wisdom and contemplate, that does not make it superior to wisdom. (Wisdom

---

[91] For a full discussion, see Gottlieb (2009, 92–111), and on problems about uniting the large-scale virtues (2009, 215–218).

[92] Here I am drawing on Devereux (2014).

[93] Cf. Rowe (1971, 112–113).

[94] See Gottlieb (2009, 99–102).

does not tell us what the virtues of character are or what they should do.) I shall elaborate this point when revisiting happiness.

At the end of the final book of the *Eudemian Ethics*, Aristotle appears to raise the same problem as appears at the beginning of this common book, but his conclusion is that the service and contemplation of the god is the standard (*horos*), a conclusion that appears to be at odds with the autonomy of thoughtfulness in this common book.[95] I shall return to this issue when I discuss the treatments of happiness in the final books of both *Eudemian* and *Nicomachean* works.

7 *Akrasia* and Pleasure

The third of the common books concerns *akrasia* and pleasure. The lengthy discussion of *akrasia* is not duplicated elsewhere, although there are comments on the topic in *Nicomachean Ethics* I 13 and in the *Eudemian* discussion of the voluntary.[96] By contrast, pleasure is the topic of half of a whole book in the *Nicomachean Ethics* (X). I shall therefore discuss the two treatments of pleasure together.

7.1 *Akrasia*

First, *akrasia*. This is a familiar phenomenon, but how is it possible to be akratic, namely, to act knowingly against one's better judgment? Aristotle aims to answer this question in the light of Socrates's claim that it is impossible to do so because nothing is stronger than knowledge, and knowledge cannot be dragged about like a slave. The discussion starts with various puzzles. For example, can people who have the virtue of thoughtfulness be akratic? Do people who act against their better judgment when it happens to be wrong act akratically, what modern philosophers call "inverse *akrasia*"? Do people who have the wrong view about what is best but act against it count as virtuous? (This sophistic type of puzzle is reminiscent of those at the beginning of *EE* VIII.) Aristotle addresses all these issues, and much more, in the following chapters.[97]

Chapter 3 of *EE* VI/*EN* VII has garnered most attention as providing Aristotle's considered analysis of *akrasia*, although commentators do not agree on what that is. In broad strokes, Aristotle begins by distinguishing different ways in which one might have knowledge. One can have knowledge without using it. One can have knowledge of universals without having

---

[95] See Devereux (2014).

[96] We have already met the akratic as someone who follows his desire versus his better judgment, and the enkratic, who follows his judgment against his desire, in earlier chapters of *EE* and *EN*.

[97] For a comprehensive discussion of the whole common book chapter by chapter, see the anthology, Natali (2009).

knowledge of particulars, and so forth. The distinction between possessing and using knowledge can also be found at the end of the account of the voluntary in *Eudemian Ethics* II 9. Aristotle's account of *akrasia* arguably makes use of his practical syllogism: While the akratic has the universal (major premise), for example, temperate people generally avoid sweets, appetite swoops in on the part of the minor premise that says "this is a sweet" so that the agent fails to put together major and minor premises and so wrongly goes after the sweet. She also fails to have the first part of the correct minor premise "I'm a temperate human being."[98] If the akratic does reach the conclusion "I should avoid the sweet," she says the words without taking them to heart.

Aristotle concludes that what he has said is what Socrates is looking for, because only perceptual knowledge is dragged about. If this is not just a disingenuous remark, one might argue that this deferential attitude to Socrates is more common in the *Eudemian* books.

7.2 Pleasure

Dorothea Frede (2006) says that Aristotle's treatment of pleasure is worthy of a Nobel prize, and it has caught the attention of philosophers from Ryle to Rawls. For Ryle (1953), it is the basis for criticizing the view of pleasure as being a quantifiable sensation, or as a separate phenomenon from the activity one is enjoying. For Rawls (1971, 426), it is the basis of his "Aristotelian Principle": "other things being equal, human beings enjoy the exercise of their realized capacities (their innate or trained abilities), and this enjoyment increases the more the capacity is realized, or the greater its complexity."

In his *Rhetoric*, Aristotle defines pleasure and pain as follows: "Let it be assumed by us that pleasure is a certain process (*kinēsis*) of the soul, an intense and perceptible settling down into its natural state and pain the opposite" (*Rh.* I 11 1369b33-35). Whether or not this definition applies to all of the pleasures and pains he discusses in the *Rhetoric*, it is a commonplace of earlier philosophers and medical writers, and seems to be Aristotle's target in both books on pleasure.[99]

According to Aristotle, pleasure (or enjoyment) is not a process or a coming-into-being (*EE* VI/*EN* VII 12 1153a9-16). Pleasure is not quick or slow like a process (*EN* X 3 1173a31-b20). Furthermore, while the process model arguably fits the pleasure of eating where one refills one's stomach, it does not apply to pleasures that are not preceded by pain, for example, the pleasure of doing mathematics or seeing (*EN* X 1173b14-22). We can enjoy activities when we are

---

[98] For a full discussion of this and the possibility of inverse *akrasia*, see Gottlieb (2021, 81–103).

[99] I owe the doubt expressed at the beginning of this sentence to Emily Fletcher.

in a natural state. In the *Eudemian* discussion of friendship, this is when we are in the mean (*EE* VII 1239b34-39).

Aristotle's positive accounts of pleasure in the common book and in the *Nicomachean Ethics*, though, have been thought to differ. In the common book, Aristotle says that pleasure is an unimpeded activity of the natural state (unimpeded, instead of perceptible) (*EE* VI/*EE* VII 12 1153a14-15), while in *Nicomachean Ethics* X, he says that "pleasure completes the activity ... as a sort of supervenient end, like the bloom on youths" (*EN* X 1174b31-33). According to Owen (1971–1972), in the common book Aristotle is talking about pleasure as in, for example, "gaming is one of my pleasures," while in *Nicomachean Ethics* X, he is talking about "getting pleasure out of gaming." Against Owen, Irwin comments on the common book, "Probably he [Aristotle] means not that the pleasure taken in running is the unimpeded activity of running, but that the pleasure is an unimpeded activity additional to the running" (Irwin 2019, 310, also Shields 2011).

For Ryleans and those who believe in Ockham's razor, there is a third alternative, summarized by Kenny:

> It is true that Aristotle prefers to speak of the activity as being a pleasure in AE <the common books> and of the pleasure arising from the activity in NE: but this does not mark a difference in doctrine. It simply means that when he talks of "activity" in NE he is often talking of impeded activities as well as unimpeded ones. The pleasure supervenes on the activity to the extent that if you say an activity is pleasant you are saying more than that it is an activity of a specific kind: but you are not saying any more than that it is a good, unimpeded, activity of that specific kind. (Kenny 2016, 236)

Therefore, when one is exercising the capacities for sense perception or thinking and doing it well, that activity, not an extra one, will be pleasant, just as, according to Aristotle, young people in the prime of life have a (supervenient) healthy glow (*EN* X 1174b31-33).[100] This view has an added bonus. Happiness, exercising one's thought and feelings well, though not identical with pleasure, will nevertheless be pleasant.[101]

There is one part of the argument in the common book that is confusing. In distinguishing types of pleasures, Aristotle suggests that recovering from an illness (a process) is only incidentally pleasant, and that the pleasure is the activity of the healthy part. Presumably Aristotle would also think that in eating,

---

[100] When the good person is engrossed in an activity and doing it well, the activity will be pleasant, just as athletes, engrossed in an activity, are "in the zone" or experience the phenomenon of "flow." On this, see Rudebusch (2009, 413–414) and Csikzentmihaly (2014).

[101] On complications regarding happiness and the pleasant life, see Gottlieb (2021, 113–117) with Frede (2009). For more on pleasure, see Gosling and Taylor (1982) and Wolfsdorf (2013).

the processes of eating are only incidentally pleasant, and that it is the exercise of taste, touch, and smell that are the enjoyable activities. In general, Aristotle's discussion of the difference between pleasures is unduly complicated here. Enter the doctrine of the measure.

According to Aristotle, the good person is the standard and measure (*kanōn kai metron*) of what is pleasant (*EN* X 5 1176a17-18). The doctrine, whose terminology is specific to the *Nicomachean Ethics*, also appeared in *EN* III 4, where Aristotle criticized Socrates's view of wish.[102] In *Nicomachean Ethics* X, Aristotle has just argued that different things are pleasurable to different species, and furthermore that different humans enjoy different things, points not made in the common book on pleasure. The measure doctrine thus not only avoids the complicated maneuvers of the common book but has the added advantage of highlighting the qualitative as opposed to merely quantitative differences between different pleasures which is what makes some good and others bad. Here Aristotle foreshadows J. S. Mill, who replaces Bentham's quantitative measurement of pleasures for a qualitative one, to be decided by those with experience and knowledge.[103]

8 Friendship

No other subject receives as much attention in Aristotle's *Eudemian* and *Nicomachean Ethics* as friendship (*philia*). There is one book on the topic in the *Eudemian Ethics* and two books in the *Nicomachean Ethics*. The short discussion that follows is not because the topic does not deserve further consideration, but because it is full of ideas that deserve a whole separate book! However, Aristotle does not discuss particular virtues of character in these pages.

Both the *Eudemian* and *Nicomachean* treatments follow the method of *endoxa* and begin with a survey of opinions on the topic. Friendship covers a variety of relationships, including those between acquaintances, friends, lovers, family members, and fellow citizens.

In his *Nicomachean Ethics*, Aristotle says that to be a friend (a) one must have goodwill toward the friend, that is, wish goods to the friend for the friend's own sake, (b) the goodwill must be reciprocated, and (c) each friend must be aware of their friend's goodwill (*EN* I VIII 2). Therefore, according to Aristotle, you

---

[102] See Gottlieb (1991; 1993). Here I explained the doctrine with reference to the difference between the unqualified goods (goods *haplōs*) and those goods that are merely good for a particular person, a distinction to be found obscurely in the *Eudemian Ethics*. I argued that the unqualified goods are ones for which it is worth getting into a condition in which they are good for oneself. (This conclusion was drawn from discussion with Peter Railton.)

[103] For Mill, see Sher (2001).

cannot be friends with an inanimate object, or a celebrity who does not know you. Aristotle makes three other important points about friendship. First, it takes time to become a friend (*EN* VIII 3 1156b25-28). Second, friends share activities (*EN* VIII 12). Third, reciprocal loving requires (good) choice (*EN* VIII 5 1157b34-35).

Aristotle distinguishes three types of friendship (*EN* VIII 3): friendship based on pleasure, friendship based on utility, and friendship based on virtue of character. The first two cases resemble the last, because good friends are pleasant and useful as well as good (*EN* VIII 4 1156b35-1157a2). Only in the last case of friendship does each friend wish goods to the friend for the friends' own sake, and not coincidentally (*EN* VIII 4 1156b9-11).[104]

It is a matter of controversy whether Aristotle's three criteria for the correct attitude to be a friend are satisfied by each type of friendship. Can people who are not virtuous satisfy the criteria, and if not, are they not really friends at all?

In the *Eudemian Ethics*, Aristotle explains the relationship between the three types of friendship more precisely than in the *Nicomachean Ethics*. The three types of friendship are not species of one genus, but nor do they merely share the same name. Instead, friendships based on pleasure and utility are related to the friendship based on virtue of character, which is primary. Aristotle explains that the relationship between friendships based on pleasure and utility and the primary case of friendship is like the relationship between, for example, a medical instrument or medical operation and a medical doctor. The former two cannot be defined except by reference to the latter (*EE* VII 1236a15-22).[105]

Aristotle stresses that the primary friendship is not a universal. It does not cover all types of friendship. Therefore, we should not expect its definition exactly to fit the other kinds of friendship. However, this does not mean that they are not friendships at all. Therefore, bad people can be friends of the first two kinds, even with good people, even if they cannot have friendships based on virtuous character (*EE* VII 1236b10-16, 1238b1-14).

Aristotle is perhaps famous for the claim, made in both works, that a friend is "another oneself." While this may sound egocentric, it is not when you realize that you are also the other self of your friend. Each work describes in more and different detail the relationship between friends: Friends enjoy perceiving one another's good qualities and gain self-knowledge by interacting with each other, as opposed to disclosing knowledge about themselves to others as emphasized

---

[104] I defend the view that one cares for the friend for the very friend's sake and not derivatively from a concern for a general property of goodness, in Gottlieb (2009, 146–150), addressing "Impersonal Friends" of Whiting (2016).

[105] A similar point about the priority of substance is made in Aristotle's *Metaphysics* IV 2 and dubbed "focal meaning" by Owen (1979).

by Kant.[106] The *Nicomachean Ethics* distinguishes two kinds of self-love. The good kind is where one gratifies one's understanding (*nous*), but, significantly, does not want to be a god (*EN* IX 4 and 8). The *Eudemian Ethics* also emphasizes the difference between humans and the god. After a long discussion considering all the pros and cons, he concludes that just because the god does not need friends does not mean that humans do not need them, because our well-being, unlike the god's, depends on something other than ourselves (*EN* VII 12 1245b13-19).

There is nothing about the possibility of friendship between humans and nonhuman animals in the *Nicomachean Ethics*, but in the *Eudemian Ethics*, Aristotle says that a human can have a friendship of utility to a small degree with a domestic animal (*EE* VII 1236b8).[107]

The *Eudemian Ethics* is noteworthy in introducing the phenomenon of civic friendship, based on equality (*EE* VII 1242b23-1243a2). There are two types of civic friendship for utility: one based on law, and one based on the fair-minded character of the people. Here Aristotle seems to favor a more democratic form of government than the monarchy he says is best in the *Nicomachean Ethics* (*EN* VIII 10).

9 Sophistic Puzzles, the *Kaloskagathos*, and Luck

Book VIII of the *Eudemian Ethics* is a fragment, with a self-contained Latin translation.[108] It begins with puzzles arising if one wrongly thinks of virtues of character and thoughtfulness as *epistēmai*, here meaning skills. The tenor of these puzzles is similar to the sophistic puzzle at the beginning of common book *EE* VI/*EN* VII and seems related to the views of Socrates.

Next Aristotle discusses the *kaloskagathos*, the beautiful-and-good person. *Kalokagathia* is noted only twice in the *Nicomachean Ethics*, once in relation to the magnanimous person (*EN* IV 1124a4), and once in contrast to the hoi polloi (*EN* X 91179b10). Unlike the merely good person, the *kaloskagathos*'s aim in being virtuous is not the natural goods, for example, wealth, honor, and physical prowess. He does virtuous acts for their own sake.[109] The existence of a merely good person is puzzling. Why won't someone whose final aim is natural goods be tempted to act viciously? Perhaps, like those who have civic bravery, which is not true bravery, they will just be lucky if acting virtuously always brings the natural goods they desire.

---

[106] See Veltman (2004) and Gottlieb (2020).

[107] This point is missed by the authors of recent articles on animal ethics based on friendship: Frööding and Peterson (2011) and Rowlands (2011).

[108] See Rowe (forthcoming).

[109] Gottlieb (2009, 145–146).

In any event, the next topic of *EE* VIII is luck, not the type of luck Solon was worrying about, which, as we saw, Aristotle discussed at greater length in his *Nicomachean Ethics* I and barely mentioned in *Eudemian Ethics* I, but luck pertaining to whether one can get on in life without being rational. The arguments take many twists and turns and are difficult to follow.[110] God and Socrates make appearances. Aristotle concludes that good luck is fortune for two sorts of nonrational people, ones successful in accord with their impulse, the others successful against their impulses.

I venture to suggest that the concern of this part of the text comes from a worry that would naturally come about if one considered that there could be reliably mean conditions that do not involve thought, the temperamental means of the *Eudemian Ethics*. But in the *Nicomachean Ethics*, those of these conditions that are reliable count as virtues of character proper and therefore require thoughtfulness. In the common book *EE* V/*EN* VI, Aristotle rightly notes that the truly natural virtues (to which these temperamental means are said to contribute at *EE* III 7 1234a25-28) are not just unreliable but harmful without understanding (*nous*) (*EE* V/*EN* VI 13 1144b9).

10 Happiness Revisited

Aristotle revisits the topic of happiness in the final book of the *Nicomachean Ethics* and briefly at the end of the final book of the *Eudemian Ethics* (*EN* X 6 1176a30–8 1179a32; *EE* VIII 1249a21-1249b25).[111]

In *Nicomachean Ethics* X, Aristotle starts by highlighting the importance of happiness as activity, a view put forward in both *Eudemian Ethics* I and *Nicomachean Ethics* I. However, in arguing for the primacy of contemplation (*theōria*), and downgrading the activities of virtues of character, he seems to forget his threefold distinction between merely instrumental goods, goods choiceworthy for their own sakes and for the sake of something else, and goods choiceworthy only for their own sake (happiness) (*EN* I 7 1097a25-1097b6). Self-sufficiency also seems to be explained in a different way from *Nicomachean Ethic* I. In book I, self-sufficiency was not defined as independence from other people. Quite the reverse (*EN* I 7 1097b8-11). In book X, the wise person is said to be self-sufficient in needing goods and friends less than do other people, although, Aristotle adds, perhaps even he will study better with others (*EN* X 7 1177a27-1177b1). Understanding (*nous*), here restricted to the understanding needed for contemplation (as opposed to any type of understanding needed for practical thinking), is singled out and even identified with the

---

[110] For a recent attempt to disentangle them, see Buddensiek (2012).

[111] On the *Nicomachean* account, see Gottlieb (2009, 59–63, 195–197; 2021, 140–142).

individual.[112] Contemplation is the best kind of happiness, but there is a caveat. Since humans are incapable of continuous contemplation, they will still need virtues of character for the rest of life. The best life humans are capable of, then, will include activities other than contemplation.

In second place come actions in accord with virtue of character and thoughtfulness, the two being yoked together. The discussion goes back and forth, returning to contemplation, self-sufficiency, and the thought that the wise person will be most loved by the gods. There is also an excursus on the gods not needing virtues of character, a strange discussion, since it does not apply to the gods of Greek myth who certainly do, nor to Aristotle's own god who is splendidly alone.[113]

In view of these anomalies, the most charitable way to read this discussion is as aporetic, presenting different views that may not all be Aristotle's. So many different ideas are presented here that the secondary literature is bursting with different interpretations.[114] There is also disagreement about what contemplation is.[115]

Indeed, in a startling aside to the reader, although one in line with the aporetic nature of his discussion, Aristotle says:

> While these sorts of considerations carry some conviction, the truth about practical matters is judged from <our> actions and way of life (*ek tōn ergōn kai tou biou*), since that is the deciding factor (*to kurion*). Hence we ought to examine what has been said by applying it to <our> actions and way of life, and if it chimes with what we do, we should accept it, but if it conflicts we should count it <mere> words. (*EN* X 8 1179a18-22)

I have argued elsewhere that Aristotle's ranking of lives in the abstract is inconsistent with his doctrine of the mean. If happiness is doing well, and doing well for a particular individual depends on that individual's abilities and the particular situations she finds herself in, it makes no sense to give a ranking of happy lives in the abstract. I therefore referred to *Politics* VII 2–3 and 15 to argue that the ranking is meant first and foremost for legislators, who are to

---

[112] Rowe (2022) argues that *sophia* (wisdom) is different in the *EE* and *EN*, entailing that *nous* (understanding) is too.

[113] On the oddity of this discussion, see too Nussbaum (1986, 373–377), and compare the passages cited earlier in my discussion of friendship.

[114] Classic discussions include Gauthier and Jolif (1958), Hardie (1967), Ackrill (1974), Kenny (1978), Devereux (1981), Keyt (1983), Irwin (1985), Whiting (1986), Roche (1988), White (1988), Kraut (1989), Broadie (1991), Reeve (1992), Crisp (1994), Lawrence (1997; 2005), Charles and Scott (1999), Lear (2004), and Irwin (2007–2009, 122–133). Cooper has changed his mind twice (Cooper 1975; 1987; 2004, 272–308).

[115] See, for example, Walker (2018) who treats contemplation as reflection on the ethical, and Curzer (2012, 394–401).

arrange the city and its education to make a happy life for its citizens.[116] (I reassess part of this view next.)

At the end of his *Eudemian Ethics,* Aristotle explains that the excellent person (*ho spoudaios*), like the physician, needs a standard (*horos*). Without that, it is like saying that nutrition is what medicine and thought (*logos*) says, which is true, but not clear. Aristotle concludes that the standard (*horos*) for the good person is "the service and contemplation of the god." Whatever promotes this is best.[117] Whatever prevents this due to deficiency or excess is bad. Assuming that the service and contemplation of the god is happiness, although Aristotle does not say so in so many words, this would seem to be another treatment of the subject matter of *Nicomachean Ethics* X.

While Aristotle seems to be addressing the same problem posed at the beginning of the common book *EE* V/*EN* VI, and with the same terminology, whether his view is compatible with what is said in the rest of that book and in *Nicomachean Ethics* X is controversial. The discussion itself is hard to follow. In outline, Aristotle seems to be arguing that as slaves serve their masters, so the governed part (the nonrational part?) of a human being serves the governing part (the rational part?). He goes on to mention the "contemplative part" (*to theōrētikon*).[118] We would expect Aristotle to continue discussing the governing part as part of the human being, whatever that is. Instead, Aristotle now refers to the god as the superior.[119]

Some commentators, followed by Walzer and Mingay (1991), have amended the text to say not "the god" but "the divine in us," avoiding the apparent non sequitur in the text and making the *Eudemian Ethics* line up with Aristotle's comments in the *Nicomachean Ethics* X, where (theoretical) understanding is described as "divine." Rowe (forthcoming a) returns to the unanimous manuscript readings. Perhaps Aristotle is instead referring to Socrates's "service to the god," as mentioned in Plato's *Apology* and *Euthyphro*, but, on its face, this is puzzling. Socrates took his divine mission to be proving the oracle wrong that he was the wisest person by carrying on philosophical conversation with anyone who would take part. This does not seem to fit with Aristotle's account of developing virtues of character in either work, nor with Aristotle's discussion of contemplation in the common book *EE* V/*EN* VI.

---

[116] Gottlieb (2009, 196–197).

[117] The text is confusing, suggesting that whatever promotes contemplation is the standard.

[118] Rowe argues that this is not the contemplative part of the soul as explained in *Nicomachean Ethics* X, but is more inclusive. He cites *EE* II 10 1226b25-26 to give its *Eudemian* credentials (notes to Rowe forthcoming).

[119] It is generally assumed that the god here is Aristotle's god, who contemplates himself, as described in *Metaphysics* XII 9 1074b15-34, and caricatured in *Magna Moralia* II 15 1212b34-1213a8.

There is a further problem. It is unclear whether Aristotle is only referring to the standard as applying to natural goods (following on from the discussion of the *kaloskagathos*), or whether it applies to actions also. Although Aristotle does talk of the actions and choices (*praxeis kai haireseis* [not *prohaireseis*]) relating to natural goods, a view I accept below, the idea that actions are good or bad if they promote contemplation or prevent us from contemplating the god is at first sight hard to square with a serious commitment to the Aristotelian virtues of character. (Why not do vicious actions if these would promote contemplation?) The view that the "service to the god" is the activity of virtue of character therefore has appeal.[120] However, its introduction via Socrates, as mentioned above, is unwarranted. Aristotle may simply be explaining that service to the god is not like the service of a slave to a master, where the master benefits. Therefore, when Aristotle says that the standard is contemplating the god, and then switches to saying that it is serving the god and contemplating, since "and" can mean "i.e." in Greek, Aristotle is explaining that serving the god just is contemplating the god.

Let us return to the question whether this whole discussion is compatible with *EE* V/*EN* VI, where thoughtfulness was the correct thought and apparently did not need any further standard.[121] In the *Eudemian Ethics*, Aristotle says that god is not a ruler who issues commands, but thoughtfulness prescribes <things> for the sake of god. He explains that "for the sake of" is said in two ways: the god is not a beneficiary, but the goal.[122]

This, while true, is less helpful than considering two other ways in which thoughtfulness may be thought to do prescribing, one where it aims to maximize contemplation of the god, and one where it prescribes when and where certain actions and contemplation should be carried out compatibly with the virtues of character. According to the first option, what the mean is in any situation depends on the contemplation it produces. On the second, when and where contemplation should be carried out depends on the agent's abilities and circumstances according to the doctrine of the mean.

If Aristotle takes the first option in the *Eudemian Ethics* (as the Latin translator clearly does), what we might consider unethical activities might be the right ones to do, as I mentioned earlier.[123] If he takes the second option, contemplation may still be a superior activity, but thoughtfulness (which, according to *EE* V/*EE* VI, cannot exist without virtue of character) is decisive in how contemplation should be arranged in a happy life. It would not be

---

[120] Kenny (2011, 188; 2016, 178). [121] Devereux (2014).

[122] On the distinction between two senses of "for the sake of," see Gottlieb and Sober (2017, 265).

[123] Aristotle's obscure final remark that the best standard is for the soul to have the least awareness of its other part as such (presumably, the nonrational part insofar as it is not responding to thought), might be thought to support this interpretation (*EE* VIII 3 1249b22-23).

appropriate to contemplate when one's friend needs help, for example, even though not helping would provide an opportunity for contemplation.[124] Whether that is what Aristotle means in either of his ethical treatises, including the final paragraph of *EN V/EE VI*, it is a much more plausible view, and it would even make Aristotle's ranking in *Nicomachean Ethics* X compatible with an individual's application of the doctrine of the mean after all.

Conclusion

I have discussed philosophically interesting similarities and differences between the *Eudemian* and *Nicomachean Ethics* throughout this Element, and so am not going to recapitulate them all here.[125] However, here are a few concluding reflections.

The trajectories of the *Eudemian* and *Nicomachean Ethics* are remarkably similar. We start off with a preliminary account of happiness, according to which happiness is exercising one's thought, desires, and feelings, according to virtue. To understand virtue of character, we need to understand choice, so Aristotle next gives an account of the voluntary and choice, followed by an account of the particular virtues of character. Both works then discuss friendship, because friends are arguably the greatest external good. While the *Eudemian Ethics* discusses various puzzles, the character of the *kaloskagathos*, and luck, the *Nicomachean Ethics,* has a nuanced discussion of pleasure.

If we add the common books, justice follows the account of particular virtues, with fair-mindedness providing a bridge from the virtues of character to the virtues of thought described at the end of the next book. Aristotle's discussion of practical reasoning leads naturally to a discussion of *akrasia*, which is accompanied by a nuanced discussion of pleasure.

There are also some apparent differences. In the *Nicomachean Ethics*, sympathetic consideration plays a more prominent part in the discussion of the voluntary and in the particular virtue of calmness, which perhaps suggests a *Nicomachean* origin for the discussion of fair-mindedness and the political virtues of thought in the common books. However, the discussions about those

---

[124] Gottlieb (1996) argues that the good person would not want to contemplate in such a situation, and so would not be making any sacrifice.

[125] It might be thought that the differences between the *Eudemian* and *Nicomachean Ethics* are due simply to their having different audiences, for example, potential philosophers in the *Eudemian Ethics* as opposed to future legislators in the *Nicomachean Ethics*, but this is already to make significant philosophical assumptions about how to understand the first and final books of each work. Leaving aside the problem of the audiences for the common books, there is a slippery slope in discussing different audiences. Tessitore (1996), for example, argued that there are different audiences for different parts of the *Nicomachean Ethics* alone. For my review of his book, see Gottlieb (1997). Thanks to William Wians for raising this issue. For more on audiences, see Scott (2020).

traits are not incompatible with what preceded these books in the *Eudemian Ethics*.[126]

The *Nicomachean Ethics* emphasizes the nonquantitative nature of happiness and the nonquantitative nature of the ethical doctrine of the mean: Happiness is not a good that can be counted as one good among many, and the doctrine of the mean does not entail that one's character can be in a mean, disposed to hit the mean in feelings and actions, merely if one has a moderate temperament, as may be suggested by the *Eudemian* discussion of temperamental means and the specific *Eudemian* worries about luck.

Consistently with this train of thought, in *EE* V/*EN* VI, one cannot have virtue of character without thoughtfulness, nor can one have thoughtfulness without virtue of character. The good person must be disposed to both feel and act as he should, when he should and so forth, as thoughtfulness prescribes. Anything less may be harmful. Therefore, the good person will have to transcend whatever temperament she was born with.[127] Consistent with this, although rather obscurely stated at the end of *EE* V/*EN* VI, contemplation is not something to be maximized but something that the good person with thoughtfulness will arrange as best she can in her life, depending on her particular abilities and the situations she finds herself in, compatibly with the doctrine of the mean. We do not find out what to do from a practical point of view by listening to the dictates of theoretical reason. The final chapter of the final book of the *Eudemian Ethics* seems to point in the same direction.

This reading of the happy life and contemplation has an important corollary. It explains why Aristotle discusses each virtue of character as he does, explaining how each virtue of character is in a mean between vices, and the characteristic feelings and actions of those who have each virtue, rather than, as students often expect, explaining how each virtue fits into an independently delineated happy life. Those whose characters are in a mean and who have thoughtfulness choose correctly based on the virtues of character they have about what to do and which goals to pursue in particular situations.

Last, but not least, in his *Nicomachean Ethics*, and following from his emphasis on the nonquantitative aspect of the doctrine of the mean, Aristotle is rightly less sanguine about temperamental means having the reliability of virtues proper. Instead, friendliness, truthfulness and wit are virtues proper. He calls these "nameless," along with calmness and the virtue concerned with honor on a small scale. I have presented various possible reasons for the namelessness of these virtues throughout this Element, but I should now like

---

[126] As I have noted, the book *EN* V/*EN* VI contains distinctions not adhered to in either of the *Eudemian* and *Nicomachean Ethics* elsewhere.

[127] This view seems to be at odds with Leunissen (2017).

to add what is maybe the most telling. In his biological works, when Aristotle says that a kind of animal is nameless, it is because he is the first to recognize it as an important explanatory classification, for example, animals with lungs (e.g., *Parts of Animals* III 6 669b10). By calling the nameless virtues "nameless," Aristotle is drawing attention to their importance, which has been overlooked. The nameless virtues combine the tact and civility needed for people to have the type of civic friendship to thrive in any society, and the diplomacy to get on with other societies too. That is why these virtues should be front and center in any ethic of virtue. It is only when these virtues are lacking in everyday and in political life that we can see how important they are.

Given the difficulty of the texts, the aforementioned reflections are inevitably speculative. Whatever conclusions are the right ones to be drawn from my earlier sections, Aristotle's thought-provoking variations on the themes of virtue and happiness make him the quintessential virtue ethicist.[128]

---

[128] On neo-Aristotelian virtue ethics, see Anscombe (1958), Foot (1978; 2001), Sherman (1997), Hursthouse (1999), and Annas (2011).

Glossary of Key Terms

English–Greek

Activity, exercise	*Energeia*
Anger, spirit	*Thumos*
Appetite	*Epithumia*
Beautiful	*Kalon*
Calmness	*Praotēs*
Choice	*Prohairesis*
Comprehension	*Sunesis*
Consideration	*Gnōmē*
Disposition	*Hexis*
Fair-mindedness	*Epieikeia*
Feelings	*Pathē*
Function	*Ergon*
Habituation, practice	*Ethismos*
Happiness	*Eudaimonia*
Impression, imagination	*Phantasia*
Pleasure	*Hēdonē*
Psyche, soul	*Psuchē*
Skill	*Technē*
Sympathetic consideration	*Suggnōmē*
Sympathy	*Eleos*
Thought	*Logos*
Thoughtfulness	*Phronēsis*
Understanding (may be practical or theoretical depending on the context)	*Nous*
Virtue	*Aretē*
Wisdom	*Sophia*
Wish	*Boulēsis*

Greek–English

Aretē	Virtue
Boulēsis	Wish
Eleos	Sympathy
Energeia	Activity, exercise

Epieikeia	Fair-mindedness
Epithumia	Appetite
Ergon	Function
Ethismos	Habituation, practice
Eudaimonia	Happiness
Gnōmē	Consideration
Hēdonē	Pleasure
Hexis	Disposition
Kalon	Beautiful
Logos	Thought
Nous	Understanding (may be practical or theoretical depending on the context)
Pathē	Feelings
Phantasia	Impression, imagination
Phronēsis	Thoughtfulness
Praotēs	Calmness
Prohairesis	Choice
Psuchē	Psyche, soul
Sophia	Wisdom
Suggnōmē	Sympathetic consideration
Sunesis	Comprehension
Technē	Skill
Thumos	Anger, spirit

References

Ackrill, John L. (1972). "Aristotle on 'Good' and the *Categories*." In Barnes, Schofield, and Sorabji (1977), 17–24.

(1973). *Aristotle's Ethics*. Translation with Notes. New York: Humanities Press.

(1974). "Aristotle on *Eudaimonia*." In Rorty (1980), 15–33.

Allan, Donald J. (1961). "Quasi-Mathematical Method in the *Eudemian Ethics*." In *Aristote et les Problèmes de Méthode*, edited by S. Mansion. Louvain: Publications Universitaires, 303–318.

Anagnostopoulos, Georgios. (ed.) (2009). *A Companion to Aristotle*. Oxford: Wiley-Blackwell.

Annas, Julia. (2011). *Intelligent Virtue*. Oxford: Oxford University Press.

Anscombe, G. E. M. (1957). *Intention*. Oxford: Blackwell.

(1958). "Modern Moral Philosophy." *Philosophy* 33: 1–19.

(1965). "Thought and Action in Aristotle." In Barnes, Schofield, and Sorabji (1977), 61–71.

Anton, Audrey. (2014). "Fixed and Flexible Characters: Aristotle on the Permanence and Mutability of Distinct Types of Character." *Society of Ancient Greek Philosophy Newsletter 2013–14*.

Baker, Samuel H. (2015). "The Concept of *Ergon*: Towards an Achievement Interpretation of Aristotle's 'Function Argument'." *Oxford Studies in Ancient Philosophy* 48: 227–266.

Barnes, Jonathan and Kenny, Anthony. (2014). *Aristotle's Ethics: Writings from the Complete Works*, revised ed. Oxford: Oxford University Press.

Barnes, Jonathan, Schofield, Malcolm, and Sorabji, Richard. (eds.) (1977). *Articles on Aristotle: Ethics and Politics*, vol. 2. London: Duckworth.

Bekker, Immanuel. (ed.) (1831). *Aristotelis Opera*, 5 vols. Berlin.

Beresford, Adam. (2020). *Aristotle: The Nicomachean Ethics*. London: Penguin.

Bobonich, Chris. (2006). "Aristotle's Ethical Treatises." In Kraut (2006), 12–29.

Brink, David O., Meyer, Susan Sauvé, and Shields, Christopher. (eds.) (2018). *Virtue, Happiness, and Knowledge: Themes from the Work of Gail Fine and Terence Irwin*. Oxford: Oxford University Press.

Broadie, Sarah. (1991). *Ethics with Aristotle*. New York: Oxford University Press.

Broadie, Sarah and Rowe, Christopher. (eds.) (2002). *Aristotle's Nicomachean Ethics*. Translation and Commentary. Oxford: Oxford University Press.

Brown, Lesley. (1997). "What Is 'the Mean Relative to Us' in Aristotle's Ethics?" *Phronesis* 42 (1): 77–93.

(2009). *Aristotle: The Nicomachean Ethics* (Oxford World's Classics). Translation by William D. Ross. Oxford: Oxford University Press.

(2014). "Why Is Aristotle's Virtue of Character a Mean? Taking Aristotle at His Word (NE ii 6)." In Polansky (2014), 64–80.

Buddensiek, Friedemann. (2012). "Does Good Fortune Matter? *Eudemian Ethics* VIII.2 on *Eutuchia*." In Leigh (2012), 155–184.

Burnet, John. (ed.) (1900). *The Ethics of Aristotle*. Introduction and Notes. London: Methuen.

Burnyeat, Myles F. (1980). "Aristotle on Learning to Be Good." In Rorty (1980), 69–92.

Bywater, Ingram. (1894). *Aristotelis Ethica Nicomachea* (Oxford Classical Text). Oxford: Clarendon Press.

Card, Claudia. (2002). *The Atrocity Paradigm: A Theory of Evil*. Oxford: Oxford University Press.

Charles, David O. M. (2012). "The *Eudemian Ethics* on the Voluntary." In Leigh (2012), 1–27.

Charles, David O. M. and Scott, Dominic. (1999). "Aristotle on Well-Being and Contemplation." *Proceedings of the Aristotelian Society* 73 (supplement): 205–223, 225–242.

Coope, Ursula. (2012). "Why Does Aristotle Think that Ethical Virtue is Required for Practical Wisdom?" *Phronesis* 57 (2): 142–163.

Cooper, John M. (1975). *Reason and Human Good in Aristotle*. Cambridge, MA: Harvard University Press.

(1987). "Contemplation and Happiness: A Reconsideration." *Synthèse* 72: 187–216.

(1999). *Reason and Emotion: Essays on Ancient Moral Psychology and Ethical Theory*. Princeton, NJ: Princeton University Press.

(2004). *Knowledge, Nature and the Human Good: Essays on Ancient Philosophy*. Princeton, NJ: Princeton University Press.

Crisp, Roger. (1994). "Aristotle's Inclusivism." *Oxford Studies in Ancient Philosophy* 12: 111–136.

(2000). *Aristotle: Nicomachean Ethics*. Cambridge: Cambridge University Press.

Csikzentmihaly, Mihaly. (2014). *Flow and the Foundations of Positive Psychology: The Collected Works of Mihaly Csikszentmihalyi*. New York: Springer.

Curzer, Howard J. (2012). *Aristotle and the Virtues*. Oxford: Oxford University Press.

Dalimier, Catherine. (2013). *Aristote Éthique à Eudème*. Traduction et presentation. Paris: Flammarion.

Devereux, Daniel T. (1981). "Aristotle on the Essence of Happiness." In *Studies in Aristotle* ed. D.J.O. Meara, Washington D.C.: Catholic University of America Press, 1981, 247–60.

Devereux, Daniel. (2014). "*Theoria* and *Praxis* in Aristotle's Ethical Treatises." In *Theoria: Studies on the Status and Meaning of Contemplation in Aristotle's Ethics (Aristote: Traductions et Etudes)*, edited by Pierre Destrée and Marco Zingano. Leuven: Peeters.

Dirlmeier, Franz. (1958). *Aristoteles, Magna Moralia, übersetzt und erlaütert*. Berlin.

Foot, Philippa. (1978). *Virtues and Vices and Other Essays in Moral Philosophy*. Berkeley, CA: University of California Press.

(2001). *Natural Goodness*. Oxford: Oxford University Press.

Fortenbaugh, William W. (1968). "Aristotle and the Questionable Mean-Dispositions." *Transactions of the American Philological Association* 99: 203–231.

Frede, Dorothea. (2006). "Pleasure and Pain in Aristotle's Ethics." In Kraut (2006), 255–275.

(2009). "*Nicomachean Ethics* VII. 11–12: Pleasure." In Natali (2009), 183–208.

(2019). "On the So-Called Common Books of the *Eudemian* and the *Nicomachean Ethics*." *Phronesis* 64 (1): 84–116.

Frede, Michael (ed.). (1987). "Categories in Aristotle." In *Essays in Ancient Philosophy*. Minneapolis, MN: University of Minnesota Press, 29–48.

Frööding, Barbara and Peterson, Martin. (2011). "Animal Ethics based on Friendship." *Journal of Animal Ethics* 1 (1): 58–69.

Gauthier, R. Antoine. and Jolif, Jean-Yves (1958). *Aristote: L'Ethique à Nicomaque*. Translation with Introduction and Commentary, 2 vols. Louvain: Publications Universitaires.

Gifford, Mark. (1995). "Nobility of Mind: The Political Dimension of Aristotle's Theory of Intellectual Virtue." In *Aristotelian Political Philosophy*, vol. 1, edited by K. J. Boudouris. Athens: International Association for Greek Philosophy, 51–60.

Gosling, Justin C. B. and Taylor, Christopher C. W. (1982). *The Greeks on Pleasure*. Oxford: Clarendon Press.

Gottlieb, Paula. (1991). "Aristotle and Protagoras: The Good Human Being as the Measure of Goods." *Apeiron* 24 (1): 25–45.

(1993). "Aristotle's Measure Doctrine and Pleasure." *Archiv für Geschichte der Philosophie* 75 (1): 31–46.

(1996). "Aristotle's Ethical Egoism." *Pacific Philosophical Quarterly* 77 (1): 1–18.

(1997). "Review of Aristide Tessitore, *Reading Aristotle's Ethics: Virtue, Rhetoric and Political Philosophy.*" *Archiv für Geschichte der Philosophie* 79: 219–220.

(2001a). *An Analysis and Discussion of Aristotle's Nicomachean Ethics I and II for Project Archelogos.* www.archelogos.com/xml/aristotleindex.htm.

(2001b). "Translating Aristotle's Ethics." *Apeiron* 34 (1): 91–99.

(2006). "The Practical Syllogism." In Kraut (2006), 218–233.

(2009). *The Virtue of Aristotle's Ethics.* Cambridge: Cambridge University Press.

(2013). "Aristotle's Ethics." In *The Oxford Handbook of the History of Ethics*, edited by Roger Crisp. Oxford: Oxford University Press, 204–272.

(2018). "Aristotle on Inequality of Wealth." In *Democracy, Justice and Equality in Ancient Greece: Historical and Philosophical Perspectives*, edited by Georgios Anagnastopoulos and Gerasimos Santas. New York: Springer, 257–268.

(2020). "Aristotle on Self-Knowledge." In *Self-Knowledge in Ancient Philosophy: The Eighth Keeling Colloquium in Ancient Philosophy*, edited by Fiona Leigh. Oxford: Oxford University Press, 130–144.

(2021). *Aristotle on Thought and Feeling.* Cambridge: Cambridge University Press.

Gottlieb, Paula and Sober, Elliott. (2017). "Nature Does Nothing in Vain." *Journal of the History of the Philosophy of Science (HOPOS)* 7 (2): 246–271.

Grant, Alexander. (1874). *The Ethics of Aristotle*, 2 vols. London: Longmans, Green.

Hardie, William Francis Ross "Frank". (1967). "The Final Good in Aristotle's Ethics." In *Aristotle: A Collection of Critical Essays*, edited by Julius M. Moravcsik . Garden City, NY: Doubleday, 297–322.

Hursthouse, Rosalind. (1999). *On Virtue Ethics.* Oxford: Oxford University Press.

(2006). "The Central Doctrine of the Mean." In Kraut (2006), 96–115.

Hutchinson, Douglas S. and Johnson, Monte R. (2017). *Aristotle's Protrepticus: Exhortation to Philosophy.* www.protrepticus.inof/protr2017x20.pdf.

Inwood, Brad and Woolf, Raphael. (eds.) (2013). *Aristotle: Eudemian Ethics.* Translation. Cambridge: Cambridge University Press.

Irwin, Terence H. (1985). "Permanent Happiness: Aristotle and Solon." *Oxford Studies in Ancient Philosophy* 3: 89–124.

(1988). *Aristotle's First Principles.* Oxford: Oxford University Press.

(2007–2009). *The Development of Ethics: A Historical and Critical Study*, 3 vols. Oxford: Oxford University Press.

(2011). "Beauty and Morality in Aristotle." In Miller (2011), 239–253.

(2019). *Aristotle: Nicomachean Ethics*. Translation with Introduction, Notes, and Glossary, 3rd ed. Indianapolis, IN: Hackett.

Jaeger, Werner W. (1923). *Aristotle: Fundamentals of the History of His Development*. Reprinted in (1962). Oxford: Oxford University Press.

(1957). "Aristotle's Use of Medicine as a Model of Method in His Ethics." *Journal of Hellenic Studies* 77: 54–61.

Jimenez, Marta. (2021). *Aristotle on Shame and Learning to Be Good*. Oxford: Oxford University Press.

Joachim, Harold H. (1951). *Aristotle: The Nicomachean Ethics*. A Commentary, edited by David A. Rees. Oxford: Clarendon Press.

Jost, Lawrence. (2014). "The *Eudemian Ethics* and Its Controversial Relationship to the *Nicomachean Ethics*." In Polansky (2014), 410–427.

Kamtekar, Rachana. (2017). *Plato's Moral Psychology: Intellectualism, the Divided Soul, and the Desire for Good*. Oxford: Oxford University Press.

Kennedy, George. (1991). *Aristotle: On Rhetoric – A Theory of Civic Discourse*. Translation with Introduction, Notes, and Appendices. Oxford: Oxford University Press.

Kenny, Anthony. (1978). *The Aristotelian Ethics: A Study of the Relationship between the Eudemian and the Nicomachean Ethics of Aristotle*. Oxford: Clarendon Press.

(1979). *Aristotle's Theory of the Will*. New Haven, CT: Yale University Press.

(2011). *Aristotle: The Eudemian Ethics*. Translation with Notes. Oxford: Oxford University Press.

(2016). *The Aristotelian Ethics: A Study of the Relationship between the Eudemian and the Nicomachean Ethics of Aristotle*. Oxford: Clarendon Press (with two reconsiderations of the first edition).

Keyt, David. (1983). "Intellectualism in Aristotle." In *Essays in Ancient Greek Philosophy IV*, edited by John P. Anton and Anthony Preus. Albany, NY: State University of New York Press, 364–387.

(2017). "Aristotle and the Joy of Working." In *Nature and Justice: Studies in the Ethical and Political Philosophy of Plato and Aristotle*. Louvain-La-Neuve: Peeters, 223–239.

Korsgaard, Christine M. (1986). "Aristotle and Kant on the Source of Value." *Ethics* 96: 486–505.

Kosman, Aryeh. (1980). "Being Properly Affected: Virtues and Feelings in Aristotle's Ethics." In Rorty (1980), 103–116.

Kraut, Richard. (1989). *Aristotle on the Human Good*. Princeton, NJ: Princeton University Press.

(ed.) (2006). *The Blackwell Guide to Aristotle's Nicomachean Ethics*. Oxford: Blackwell.

(2013). "An Aesthetic Reading of Aristotle's Ethics." In *A Festschrift for Malcolm Schofield*, edited by Verity Harte and Melissa Lane. Cambridge: Cambridge University Press, 231–250.

(2018). *The Quality of Life: Aristotle Revised*. Oxford: Oxford University Press.

Lawrence, Gavin. (1997). "Nonaggregability, Inclusiveness, and the Theory of Focal Value: *Nicomachean Ethics* I.7. 1097b16-20." *Phronesis* 42 (1): 32–76.

(2005). "Snakes in Paradise: Problems in the Ideal Life in *NE* 10." Spindel Conference 2004. *The Southern Journal of Philosophy* 43 (supplement): 126–165.

Lear, Gabriel Richardson. (2004). *Happy Lives and the Highest Good: An Essay on Aristotle's Nicomachean Ethics*. Princeton, NJ: Princeton University Press.

Lee, Mi-Kyoung (Mitzi). (in press). *Justice in Aristotle's Ethics and Political Philosophy*. Oxford: Oxford University Press.

Leigh, Fiona. (2012). *The Eudemian Ethics on the Voluntary, Friendship, and Luck: The Sixth S.V. Keeling Colloquium in Ancient Philosophy*. Boston, MA: Brill.

Leighton, Stephen R. (2011). "Inappropriate Passion." In Miller (2011), 211–236.

Leunissen, Mariska. (2017). *From Natural Character to Moral Virtue in Aristotle*. New York: Oxford University Press.

Lloyd. Geoffrey. E. R. (1968). "The Role of Medical and Biological Analogies in Aristotle's Ethics." *Phronesis* 13 (1): 68–83.

Lorenz, Hendrik. (2009a). "*NE* VII. 4: Plain and Qualified *akrasia*." In Natali (2009), 72–101.

(2009b). "Virtue of Character in Aristotle's *Nicomachean Ethics*." *Oxford Studies in Ancient Philosophy* 37: 177–252.

McDowell, John. (2009). *The Engaged Intellect: Philosophical Essays*. Cambridge, MA: Harvard University Press.

Meinwald, Constance. (2016). *Plato*. New York: Routledge.

(2017). "What are the *Philotheamones* and What are They Thinking? *Ta Polla Kala* in *Republic* V." *Ancient Philosophy* 37 (1): 39–57.

Menn, Stephen. (1995). "Metaphysics, Dialectic and the Categories." *Revue de Metaphysique et Morale* 100 (3): 311–337.

Meyer, Susan Sauvé. (2012). *Aristotle on Moral Responsibility: Character and Cause*. Oxford: Oxford University Press.

(2016). "Virtue, Goals, and *Phronesis*: Evidence from the Social and Natural Virtues." Paper presented at University of Pennsylvania and Remnin University, Beijing.

(forthcoming). *How to Flourish: An Ancient Guide to Living Well.* An abridged version of Aristotle's *Nicomachean Ethics*, selected, translated, and introduced by Susan Sauvé Meyer, Princeton University Press.

Miller, Fred D. (1995). *Nature, Justice, and Rights in Aristotle's Politics.* Oxford: Clarendon Press.

Miller, Jon. (ed.) (2011). *Aristotle's Nicomachean Ethics: A Critical Guide.* Cambridge: Cambridge University Press.

Mills, Michael J. (1985). "*Phthonos* and its Related *pathē* in Plato and Aristotle." *Phronesis* 30: 1–12.

Moss, Jessica. (2011). "Virtue Makes the Goal Right: Virtue and *Phronesis* in Aristotle's Ethics." *Phronesis* 56 (3): 204–261.

Natali, Carlo. (1999). *Aristotele: Etica Nicomachea.* Introduzione, traduzione e note. Laterza: Roma-Bari.

(2009). *Aristotle: Nicomachean Ethics, Book VII: Symposium Aristotelicum.* Oxford: Oxford University Press.

(2013). *Aristotle: His Life and School,* edited by Douglas S. Hutchinson. Princeton, NJ: Princeton University Press.

Nikolaidis, Anastasios G. (1982). "Aristotle's Treatment of the Concept of *PRAOTHS.*" *Hermes* 110 Bd. H4: 414–422.

Nussbaum, Martha C. (1986). *The Fragility of Goodness: Luck and Ethics in Greek Philosophy.* Cambridge: Cambridge University Press.

(2015). "Transitional Anger." *Journal of the American Philosophical Association* 1 (1): 41–56.

Ober, Josiah. (2013). "Political Animals Revisited." *The Good Society* 22 (2): 201–214.

Olfert, Christiana M. M. (2017). *Aristotle on Practical Truth.* Oxford: Oxford University Press.

Owen, Gwilym E. L. (1960). "Logic and Metaphysics in Some Early Works of Aristotle." In Nussbaum (1986), 180–199.

(1971–1972). "Aristotelian Pleasures." In Barnes, Schofield, and Sorabji (1977), 92–103.

(1979). "Logic and Metaphysics in Some Earlier Works of Aristotle". In *Articles on Aristotle.* Vol 3. Metaphysics. (eds) Barnes, Schofield and Sorabji, London: Duckworth, 1979, 13–32.

Owen, Gwilym E. L. and Nussbaum, Martha. (eds.) (1986). *Logic, Science and Dialectic.* Cambridge: Cambridge University Press.

Pakaluk, Michael. (2011). "On the Unity of the *Nicomachean Ethics.*" In Miller (2011), 23–44.

Pears, David. (1980). "Courage as a Mean." In Rorty (1980), 171–187.

Pearson, Giles. (2012). *Aristotle on Desire*. Cambridge: Cambridge University Press.

Penner, Terrence M. I. (1987). *The Ascent from Nominalism: Some Existence Arguments in Plato's Middle Dialogues*. Dordrecht: Reidel.

Peterson, Sandra. (1992). "Apparent Circularity in Aristotle's Account of Right Action in the *Nicomachean Ethics.*" *Apeiron* 25: 83–107.

Polansky, Ronald. (ed.) (2014). *The Cambridge Companion to Aristotle's Nicomachean Ethics*. Cambridge: Cambridge University Press.

Price, Anthony W. (2011). "Aristotle on the Ends of Deliberation." In *Moral Psychology and Human Action in Aristotle*, edited by M. Pakaluk and G. Pearson. Oxford: Oxford University Press, 135–158.

Primavesi, Oliver. (2007). "Ein Blick in Den Stollen von Skepsis: Vier Kapitel Zur Frühen Uberlieferung Des Corpus Aristotelicum." *Philologus* 151 (1): 51–77.

Rackham, Harris H. (1934). *Aristotle: Nicomachean Ethics* (Loeb Classical Library, Vol. XIX). Cambridge, MA: Harvard University Press.

(1981). *The Athenian Consitution, the Eudemian Ethics, on Virtues and Vices*. Cambridge, MA: Harvard University Press.

Rawls, John. (1971). *A Theory of Justice*. Cambridge, MA: Harvard University Press.

Reeve, C. D. C. (David). (1992). *Practices of Reason*. Oxford: Oxford University Press.

(2014). *Aristotle: Nicomachean Ethics*. Translation with Introduction and Notes. Indianapolis, IN: Hackett.

Roche, Timothy D. (1988). "*Ergon* and *Eudaimonia* in *Nicomachean Ethics* I: Reconsidering the Intellectualist Interpretation." *Journal of the History of Philosophy* 26: 175–194.

Romilly, Jacqueline. (1974). "Fairness and Kindness in Thucydides." *Phoenix* (Special Edition: Studies Presented to Mary E. White on the Occasion of Her Sixty-Fifth Birthday) 28 (1): 95–100.

Rorty, Amélie O. (ed.) (1980). *Essays on Aristotle's Ethics*. Berkeley, CA: University of California Press.

Ross, William D. (1923). *Translation of Aristotle's Nicomachean Ethics*. London: Routledge, and on the web.

Rowe, Christopher. (1971). *The Eudemian and Nicomachean Ethics: A Study in the Development of Aristotle's Thought*. Cambridge: Cambridge Philological Society. Supplement no. 2.

(1975). "A Reply to John Cooper on the *Magna Moralia.*" *American Journal of Philology* 96: 160–172.

(2020). *Presentation at the III Workshop Internacional de Filosofía Antigua.* https://youtu.be/VxubkdlEWkg?t=8118

(2022). "*Sophia* in the *Eudemian Ethics*." In *Investigating the Relationship between Aristotle's Eudemian and Nicomachean Ethics*, edited by Giulio di Basilio. London: Routledge.

(forthcoming). *Aristotelis Ethica Eudemia* (Oxford Classical Text). Oxford: Clarendon Press.

Rowlands, Mark. (2011). "Friendship and Animals: A Reply to Frööding and Peterson." *Journal of Animal Ethics* 1 (1): 70–79.

Rudebusch, George. (2009). "Pleasure." In Anagnostopoulos (2009), 404–419.

Ryle, Gilbert. (1953). "Pleasure." In *Dilemmas*. Reprinted in (2015). Cambridge: Cambridge University Press, 46–57.

Sachs, Joe. (2001). *Aristotle's Nicomachean Ethics*. Translation with Glossary and Introductory Essay. Newburyport, MA: Focus/R. Pullins.

Santas, Gerasimos. (1989). "Aristotle's Criticism of Plato's Form of the Good: Ethics without Metaphysics?" *Philosophical Quarterly* 18 (2): 137–160.

Scheiter, Krisanna. (2012a). "Emotion, Imagination, and Feeling in Aristotle." PhD Dissertation. University of Pennsylvania.

(2012b). "Images, Appearances and *Phantasia* in Aristotle." *Phronesis* 57 (3): 251–278.

Schofield, Malcolm and Striker, Gisela. (eds.) (1986). *The Norms of Nature: Studies in Hellenistic Ethics*. Cambridge: Cambridge University Press.

Scott, Dominic. (2020). *Listening to Reason in Plato and Aristotle*. Oxford: Oxford University Press.

Sher, George. (2001). *J. S. Mill: Utilitarianism: and the 1868 Speech on Capital Punishment*, 2nd ed. Indianapolis, IN: Hackett.

Sherman, Nancy. (1997). *Making a Necessity of Virtue: Aristotle and Kant on Virtue*. Cambridge: Cambridge University Press.

Shields, Christopher. (1999). *Order in Multiplicity: Homonymy in the Philosophy of Aristotle*. Oxford: Oxford University Press.

(2011). "Perfecting Pleasures: The Metaphysics of Pleasure in *Nicomachean Ethics* X." In Miller (2011), 191–210.

Simpson, Peter. (2013). *The Eudemian Ethics of Aristotle*. Translation with Explanatory Commentary. London: Routledge.

Stewart, John A. (1892). *Notes on the Nicomachean Ethics*, vols. 1 and 2. Oxford: Clarendon Press.

Striker, Gisela. (2006). "Aristotle's Ethics as Political Science." In *The Virtuous Life in Greek Ethics*, edited by Burkhart Reis. Cambridge: Cambridge University Press, 127–141.

Taylor, Christopher C. W. (2006). *Aristotle: Nicomachean Ethics Books II-IV*. Translation with Introduction and Commentary. Oxford: Clarendon Press.

Tessitore, Aristide. (1996). *Reading Aristotle's Ethics: Virtue, Rhetoric and Political Philosophy.* Albany, NY: State University of New York Press.

Tredennick, Hugh and Armstrong, G. Cyril. (1935). *Oeconomica I-III, Metpahysics X-XIV, Magna Moralia I and II* (The Loeb Classical Library). Cambridge, MA: Harvard University Press.

Urmson, James O. (1973). "Aristotle's Doctrine of the Mean." In Rorty (1980), 157–170.

Veltman, Andrea. (2004). "Aristotle and Kant on Self-Disclosure in Friendship." *Journal of Value Inquiry* 38 (2): 225–239.

Walker, Matthew. (2018). *Aristotle on the Uses of Contemplation.* Cambridge: Cambridge University Press.

Walzer, Richard R. and Mingay, Jean M. (1991). *Aristotelis Ethica Eudemia* (Oxford Classical Text). Oxford: Clarendon Press.

Whiting, Jennifer. (1986). "Human Nature and Intellectualism in Aristotle." *Archiv für Geschichte der Philosophie* 68: 70–95.

(2016). *First, Second, and Other Selves: Essays on Friendship and Personal Identity.* Oxford: Oxford University Press.

White, Nicholas P. (1988). "Good as Goal." *The Southern Journal of Philosophy* 27, supplementary vol: 163–93.

Wiggins, David. (1975–1976). "Deliberation and Practical Reason." In Rorty (1980), 221–241.

Wolfsdorf, David. (2013). *Pleasure in Ancient Greek Philosophy.* Cambridge: Cambridge University Press.

Woods, Michael J. (1992). *Aristotle: Eudemian Ethics*, 2nd ed. Translation with Commentary. Oxford: Clarendon Press.

Young, Charles M. (1996). "The Doctrine of the Mean." *Topoi* 15 (1): 89–99.

Yount, David. (1998). "Plato v. Aristotle: Is the Form of the Good Relevant to Ethics?" PhD Thesis. University of Wisconsin-Madison.

Acknowledgments

First I would like to thank members of my most recent graduate seminar on Aristotle's Ethics: Mandi Adie, Burgandy Basulto, Michael Bruckner, Abiral Chitrakar Phnuyal, Marisa Considine, Patrick Cronin, Meryem Keskin, Shiying Li, Mason Peck, Alex Pho, Phillip Pinell, Andi Sirokman, Timothy Tennyson, and Elise Whatley.

Thanks also to attendees at the most recent meetings of "the Greeks": Emily Fletcher, David Hildner, Mary Krizan, Terry Penner, Naomi Reshotko, Ruth Saunders, Bjorn Wastvedt, George Wright, and Inara Zanuzzi.

I am grateful to Christopher Rowe for letting me and the Greeks have an advance copy of his forthcoming Oxford Classical Text of the *Eudemian Ethics*, with apparatus and notes.

I have benefitted from discussing the "nameless" virtues with Marta Jimenez, Monte Johnson, Susan Sauvé Meyer, Krisanna Scheiter, and Maria Vaccarezza.

Thanks to Dylan Beschoner for help in collating and formatting the bibliography, and thanks to UW-Madison for granting me a sabbatical semester to work on this Element.

I would also like to thank Ben Eggleston and Dale Miller, editors of this Cambridge Elements series, for their support, and Ben Eggleston for helpful comments. Thanks also to the two anonymous referees. Last, but not least, I would like to thank my unofficial editor, Henry, with love.

This Element is dedicated to the memory of Michael Woods, my main supervisor for the B.Phil at Oxford many years ago, and an aficionado of Aristotle's *Eudemian Ethics*.

Cambridge Elements ≡

Ethics

Ben Eggleston

University of Kansas

Ben Eggleston is a professor of philosophy at the University of Kansas. He is the editor of John Stuart Mill, *Utilitarianism: With Related Remarks from Mill's Other Writings* (Hackett, 2017) and a co-editor of *Moral Theory and Climate Change: Ethical Perspectives on a Warming Planet* (Routledge, 2020), *The Cambridge Companion to Utilitarianism* (Cambridge, 2014), and *John Stuart Mill and the Art of Life* (Oxford, 2011). He is also the author of numerous articles and book chapters on various topics in ethics.

Dale E. Miller

Old Dominion University, Virginia

Dale E. Miller is a professor of philosophy at Old Dominion University. He is the author of *John Stuart Mill: Moral, Social and Political Thought* (Polity, 2010) and a co-editor of *Moral Theory and Climate Change: Ethical Perspectives on a Warming Planet* (Routledge, 2020), *A Companion to Mill* (Blackwell, 2017), *The Cambridge Companion to Utilitarianism* (Cambridge, 2014), *John Stuart Mill and the Art of Life* (Oxford, 2011), and *Morality, Rules, and Consequences: A Critical Reader* (Edinburgh, 2000). He is also the editor-in-chief of *Utilitas*, and the author of numerous articles and book chapters on various topics in ethics broadly construed.

About the Series

This Elements series provides an extensive overview of major figures, theories, and concepts in the field of ethics. Each entry in the series acquaints students with the main aspects of its topic while articulating the author's distinctive viewpoint in a manner that will interest researchers.

Cambridge Elements ⬚

Ethics

A full series listing is available at: www.cambridge.org/EETH